ONE IN A SERIES FROM THE PUBLISHERS OF *PRE-K TODAY*

LEARNING THROUGH PLAY

LANGUAGE

A Practical Guide for Teaching Young Children

Written by Susan Miller, Ed.D.

Contributing Writers:

Ellen Booth Church

Lisa Feeney

Merle Karnes, Ed.D.

Constance Ward

Illustrated by Nicole Rubel

With great fondness to my grandmother, Emma Anderson, who inspired my passion for books as a child with wonderful bedtime stories. And to my grandfather, Wilfred Anderson, who lovingly told me stories each night in the very best oral tradition.   — *Susan Anderson Miller*

Early Childhood Division Vice President and Publisher
Helen Benham

Art Director
Sharon Singer

Art Editor
Toby Fox

Production Editor
Katie Lyons

Editors
Nancy-Jo Hereford
Jane Schall

Assistant to the Author
Karen Epting

Published by:
Scholastic Inc.
Early Childhood Division
730 Broadway
New York, NY 10003

ISBN # 0-590-49174-1

12, 11, 10, 9, 8, 7, 6, 5, 4, 3, 2   3, 4, 5, 6, 7, 8/9
33

Printed in the U.S.A.
First Scholastic printing, October 1991

CONTENTS

LEARNING
AND
GROWING
WITH LANGUAGE

ACTIVITY
PLANS
FOR TWOS, THREES, FOURS, AND FIVES

Cover Photo: James Levin

FOREWORD
The Value of Learning Language Through Play

Language is the wonder of words dancing across the page, rhyming, telling stories, bringing experiences to life. It is the power of words to express new thoughts — in conversations, giving directions, and sharing feelings. And language is the command of words to state "what's what" — signs, lists, letters, and labels. Through the eyes and the world of a young child, language opens up new powers, insights, and delights. It is the beginning of seeing life and communicating thoughts in deeper and broader ways, of getting to know others, of playing with a growing ability to express feelings.

How does language come alive to children? How does it grow and develop to become not just a lifelong skill but also a lifelong friend? The answer cannot be found in a packet of preschool worksheets or a song one teaches to memorize the alphabet. Language comes alive when children experience firsthand the power and excitement of using words to help them accomplish what they want to do. Whether this involves making a list together to remember all the things they'll need to fix banana bread for snack, dictating an I-miss-you note to Mommy, or helping to create and then post a sign that says, "My building is not finished. Please do not touch," language becomes a useful tool. And, as educators of older children are finding out, this is true not just for the very young but for children in upper grades, too. We use and love what helps us give meaning to our lives.

Learning Through Play: Language
clearly demonstrates that early childhood education and developmentally appropriate practices lead the way in this thinking. As you read through various parts of the book — sections on developing language, your role, setting up your environment, and talking with families — I am sure that it will be obvious to you (if it isn't already) that language permeates strong early childhood curriculum; that print-rich environments are natural settings for young children; and that good early childhood literature offers a rich assortment of language-growth experiences. As well, the philosophy of early childhood education — following a child's lead, building on children's ideas — is a major component of true, hands-on language development.

Susan Miller and the other contributors to this book, Ellen Booth Church, Lisa Feeney, Constance Ward, Merle Karnes, Nancy-Jo Hereford, and I, invite you to use the information, ideas, and insights here as springboards to glorious language adventures with your children. As they discover that they can use words to express their thoughts and feelings, you will be there to support the risks they take as they speak and write, and to enjoy their delight as they experience the power of communication.

—*Jane Schall*
Editor
Pre-K Today

"Language grows out of life, out of its needs and experiences ... Good work in language ... depends on a real knowledge of things."

Annie Sullivan
Teacher to Helen Keller

DEVELOPING LANGUAGE: A SKILL FOR LIFE

A baby cries and language begins. And we spend the rest of our lives communicating our joys, pleasures, pains, feelings, and needs to the world around us. Infants quickly discover the power of their language. If they cry, someone should respond. If they coo and smile, someone may coo and smile back. Language becomes interaction with others.

WHAT IS LANGUAGE?

Sounds, signs, symbols — language is a complex system. Letters combine into words. Sounds become elements of oral language. When the combinations are meaningful, they enable us to communicate with others.

A child listens: This is receptive language — communication taken in from others. A child speaks: This is expressive language — coming from within and shared with others.

But what is *whole language*? It is lis-

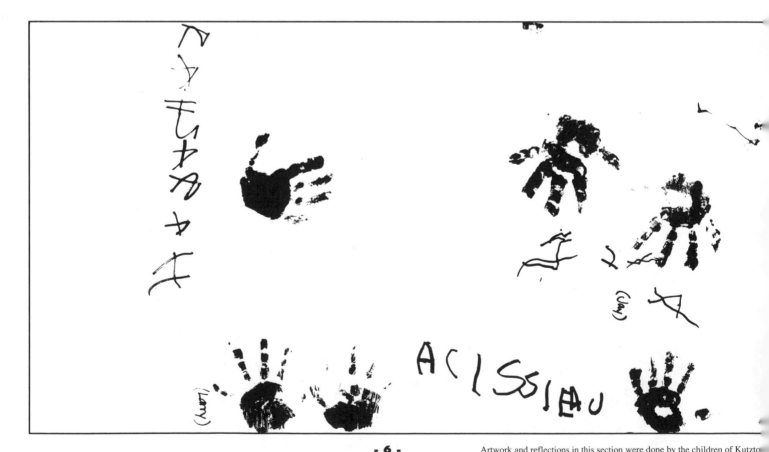

Artwork and reflections in this section were done by the children of Kutzto

tening, speaking, writing, and reading — interrelated, developing together, each as important as the other.

THE WHOLE OF WHOLE LANGUAGE

Language has the marvelous ability to foster growth in every area of a child's development. Physical, social, emotional, and cognitive development are each enhanced as a child's oral and written language develop.

■ *Physically*, a child's fine-motor skills progress from scribblings to designs, pictures, circles, and crude letters, to written "invented" words. As fine-motor skills develop, interested young readers are better able to turn the pages of a book. Gross-motor skills assist children in dramatic-play involvement as they portray story characters; when they sing songs with accompanying actions; and as they participate in music-and-movement games.

Reading, speaking, listening, and writing are all part of a child's day and part of his or her physical movement.

■ *Cognitively*, young children learn that marks stand for something (symbolic representation) as they scribble or draw pictures and then describe their artwork, or as they dictate a story for you to write down. They learn to solve problems using language, asking questions and sharing ideas. Reading predictable stories helps children anticipate what will happen as they clue into language patterns such as rhymes or repeating phrases.

Very young children point to objects and actions to find out what they're called, learning about words and concepts. Children love to classify, sort, and compare, growing in their ability to say what goes together and why. Language becomes a constant helper and a meaningful part of their world.

■ *Socially*, language enables children to whisper secrets to a special pal or send a letter to a friend who's moved away. It allows preschoolers to give voice to imaginative characters and roles during dramatic play, and enables kindergartners to engage in long dialogues with a fellow builder or partner in a project. Books are the perfect excuse for curling

"This Is Who We Are."
— A.M. Nursery
Kutztown University's
Early Learning Center

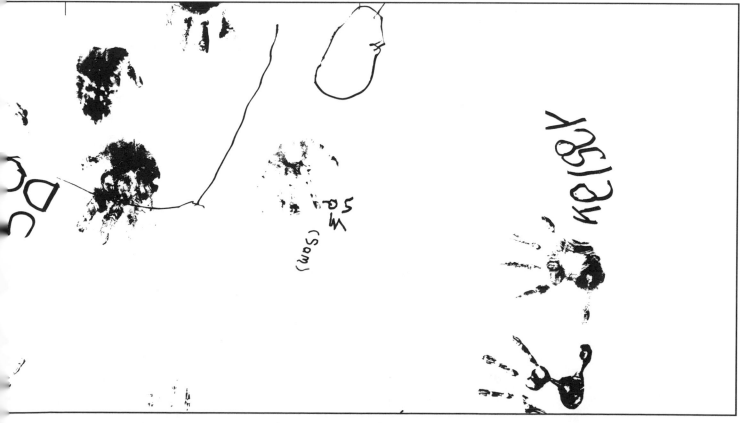

This is me walking with 100 balls. — *Jenny S.*

up on the couch and sharing a story. And as language skills increase, children get more adept at resolving conflicts in cooperative ways.

■ *Emotionally*, children use language to express their feelings. Through dramatic play, a child can vent her feelings as she pretends to tell the new baby, "Stay in your crib! Mommy wants to take Sasha to the circus." The language of literature helps children relate their fears or feelings to a book's character or plot. How many young children have identified with Ira, who really doesn't want to leave his teddy bear home when he sleeps over at his friend's house for the first time? [*Ira Sleeps Over* by Bernard Waber (Houghton Mifflin)]

WHAT HAPPENS AS LANGUAGE DEVELOPS?

As you know, language development is an ongoing process. Adults foster early language growth by singing to a baby, naming foods as she eats, encouraging her to say "bye-bye" to Grandma, and playfully tracing circles on her tummy during diapering.

As a child grows, she finds that language helps her make sense of her world and helps the people in her world make sense of her needs. With encouragement from adults, a young child becomes a language explorer, experimenting with and testing different ways to communicate, learning about language as she uses it in ways that are meaningful to her.

The importance of this simple, natural start on the road to literacy cannot be overstated. From birth to preschool, language is the foundation of so many activities and experiences. Listening and speaking are prerequisites to discussing any subject, as well as to forming bonds with peers. Reading and writing are fundamental ways of taking in new information and of sharing one's own ideas and understandings.

How comfortable children feel with language, how well they use it, and consequently, how well they communicate their own ideas and emotions and understand the ideas and emotions communicated by others, is often a predictor of how successful they'll be in school, in relationships, and in life.

This book is designed to assist you in helping the children in your program to learn language in a natural, "whole" way, and to help children love language for the joy and meaning that listening, speaking, reading, and writing bring to life.

LANGUAGE IS MORE THAN ABC

Language consists of four important components — listening, speaking, writing, and reading. Here is some information about each.

■ *Listening* — As early as the first few months of life, infants learn to listen to their caregivers' voices and take cues from their tones. Later, during toddler, preschool, and kindergarten years, children use listening skills to acquire information as well as for enjoyment.

There are many different ways to listen. Children grow in their ability to hear other sounds or requests while engaged in their own activities; to listen for information or for pleasure; and to analyze the sounds they hear.

■ *Speaking* — Infants verbalize from birth, beginning with random sounds. From one to two years of age, children most often use one-word sentences (or commands!). From two to three years, children generally speak in two- or three-word phrases, while after three, most begin to develop full speech pat-

terns. As they acquire speech, children also learn unwritten rules about how and when to use certain language — often understanding more words and nuances than they practice.

■ *Writing* is active! It's a process that involves children in expressing ideas and feelings by creating marks on paper. When children first hold crayons at about 15 months, they're most interested in the scribbling process. By preschool, scribbling becomes more controlled and deliberate drawings and designs emerge. Gradually, children attempt letterlike forms and by kindergarten age most write letter approximations. When children become interested in learning the sounds of letters, they often try to write words using invented spelling: "HM" for "home."

■ *Reading* enables children to enter new worlds. And as you know, no child is ever too young to be read to. Cuddling with a child and a good children's book is only the beginning of the positive, wondrous feelings later reading adventures will bring.

As young children are read to, they begin to understand that the marks on the page have special meaning. In a print-rich environment, they recognize that these marks are letters with special sounds. Beginning with reading her own dictation, eventually a child will write her own words, read them, and move on to recognizing and reading words in books and other places.

For a more detailed review of the skills and concepts developed through language, turn to "Learning and Growing With Language" on page 28. The sidebar "Ages and Stages," beginning on page 12, will also give you general guidelines by age.

When I grow up I want to be ENJEr (engineer)

Joshua 5

YOUR ROLE
IN FOSTERING
LANGUAGE DEVELOPMENT

In so many ways, language is the most natural of skills to develop. But to develop it well, children need strong language models. They need people in their lives who use language to communicate their thoughts, feelings, dreams, and ideas; people who listen and respond; people who write — quick notes, long letters, shopping lists; and people who read to them and also read for their own pleasure. What children see and hear they begin to imitate.

MODELING LANGUAGE: A VERY IMPORTANT ROLE

You are one of those important models — in fact, one of the most influen-

tial models. And, as you know, it's not the size of the words you use — it's your interest in language that counts. It's demonstrating an enjoyment of words as you communicate with basic good grammar. It's helping children recognize the value of listening by listening to them. It's showing delight in a good story and fascination in the magic pictures that words can create in your mind.

Naturally, there are other adults who serve as language models. And children are models for each other. But you hold a special place in children's lives. Your influence on their language development can have a lasting impact as you help them use and find pleasure in all forms of language.

WHAT ARE YOUR OTHER ROLES?

You wear many hats as a teacher of young children. Each of your various roles plays a part in helping to develop children's language. And as you well know, you exercise many of them simultaneously!

■ *Observer* — This is a very important role. By observing children, you can gain useful information about their interests, social interactions, problem-solving abilities, and vocabulary development. You can also learn ways to extend their language development. For example, you may see Sam kick the pillows in the housekeeping area, yelling, "Bad dog. Don't bite Sam!" Later, you might offer Sam a stuffed toy dog and gently encourage him to use words to work through his anger or fear.

■ *Participant* — There are times when your direct involvement in children's activities enhances not only their language but the level of play. For example, you may observe a dramatic-play scenario that has bogged down, so you ask a question to encourage creative thinking: "How do you think you might get your boat off this island?" "Is there anything you could use?" If children still need it, offer a little assistance: "Could this oar (a long wooden block) help?" Don't stay involved for too long or you risk exercising too much influence on their play. Be sensitive to children who would rather not have you participate in their play by respecting those feelings.

■ *Evaluator* — As you watch a child, analyze what you see. For example, after observing over time that a four-year-old has difficulty paying attention and seldom follows directions, you might develop a game to increase his listening and attending skills, such as clapping softly, then loudly, or quickly, then slowly, while monitoring his imitation of those sounds. Recording your observations and evaluations also provides helpful information to review

with families during conferences or at other times.

■ *Manager* — In this role, you help create and set up well-defined centers and provide children with materials they can manipulate, always stressing process over product. As you organize centers and materials, plan for a majority of small-group and one-on-one activities that encourage conversation between children and/or with you.

■ *Scheduler* — Your daily routine has a considerable impact on language development. When children feel rushed, their imagination and potential to use language are diminished. Allow for long blocks of time when children can compose on the computer in the writing center or develop a play theme in the dramatic-play area.

Remember, too, that children need a set schedule of activities, so that they know to expect a story after snack each day. Make periodic announcements about your own schedule for children who want your assistance with an activity. For example, after the story you might explain, "I'm going to the writing center now. If anyone has a story for me to write down, join me there."

Of course, acting as scheduler doesn't mean dictating children's activities. Part of growing and learning is choosing and directing their own activities, so that they're using language in ways that are meaningful to them.

■ *Reinforcer* — You acknowledge and reinforce children's attempts at language all the time. When two-year-old Willy points to the mud on his shoe and says "dity," you acknowledge his efforts and model correct pronunciation: "Yes, Willie, your shoe is dirty." When Mark realizes that the "M" you've written on the experience chart is the first letter of his name, you let him know it's great that he's made the connection and reinforce this understanding: "Yes, Mark, this 'M' is the same letter that is in your name. It sounds like 'm-m-m.'" Or you encourage a child's use of invented spelling: "Dolores, I can read your

AGES & STAGES
OF LANGUAGE DEVELOPMENT

How children acquire language depends not only on their experiences but on their age, developmental level, and interests. Use these guidelines to help gauge your children's literacy development as you observe them at play.

Two-year-olds:

- put two or three important words together: "Mommy go down."
- enjoy naming familiar objects, including body parts.
- imitate familiar observed behaviors and sounds, such as creating siren sounds for their fire trucks.
- follow simple directions.
- like to be read simple stories with large pictures. They often request favorite stories over and over and want to help turn the pages.
- like to hear and say nursery rhymes.
- begin to show a hand preference.
- draw random scribbles, and may make crude-looking circles.
- use basic pronouns by age three.

Three-year-olds:

- use three or four words in a sentence. ("Scott is sleeping.")
- know some words for colors, shapes, and counting.
- utilize plurals ("I eat apples") and comparison words ("Jean is taller").
- match words to actions ("Jon is running").
- can say their full name.
- ask lots of questions!
- enjoy repeating fingerplays and delight in nonsense rhymes with silly sounding words.
- talk with peers during dramatic play or to themselves when they play alone.
- enjoy books about friends or other familiar themes, and like to look at books alone.
- manipulate crayons and pencils and mark with a purpose in the controlled-scribbling stage.

beautiful sign — 'Beauty Shop' ('BUT SP')!"

When you ask questions about a story character, you reinforce children's understanding of the plot, their ability to make connections between story events and events in their own lives, and the value of expressing their opinions. For example, asking, "How do you think Peter felt when his furniture was painted over?" [*Peter's Chair* by Ezra Jack Keats (Harper & Row)], can lead to a discussion of how children have felt when having to give up a toy or other item to a younger sibling.

Your role as reinforcer is a positive one. Correct children's misuse of language through modeling, not by asking them to "say it right" or to "make the letter this way." Dwelling on children's errors will stifle future efforts.

■ *Guide* — When you don this hat, you help lead and extend children's language in challenging ways. For example, as a child traces over sandpaper letters in the writing center, you might ask, "I wonder if any of these letters are made with circle shapes? Let's find out." Or if Gregory wants his name printed on a card, you might assist him in matching the letters in his name with the letters on a magnetic board. And to stretch children's thinking, you can predict together what ingredients might go in Stone Soup before reading the story aloud.

To be a successful guide, follow your children's lead and build on their interests. Tune in to each child's abilities, so that the challenges you offer are ones he or she can meet and that will also help to enhance his self-esteem.

■ *Information Giver* — As you share information and knowledge with children, you demonstrate one of the key functions of language. When Matt asks how the group will get to the zoo, you respond orally, "We're traveling by bus." When you create a map with animal symbols to show children the route you'll take inside the zoo and which animals they'll see, you show them that

written language, too, is a source of useful information.

■ *Nurturer* — As you focus on children's emotional well-being, you also help to develop language. Your careful listening to an anxious child encourages him to see words as a way of communicating feelings and solving problems. When you help a homesick child "write a letter to Mommy," you demonstrate that putting words on paper can be an emotional release. And when you rock a child who's having trouble separating and read a story he can relate to, such as *Good Morning, Baby Bear* by Eric Hill (Random House), you help him discover that books can be truly wonderful companions.

MAKING LANGUAGE MEANINGFUL

When you stop to consider these different roles and the ways that each helps to develop a child's language skills, there's a common thread woven through each: All involve integrating language in ways that are meaningful to children. It's hard to overstate just how important that is.

To those who aren't aware of developmentally appropriate learning, the most important and significant ways of developing children's language skills in an early childhood setting may go unnoticed. "Where are the worksheets?" you may hear. Aren't those nice, neat pages where children find the objects that start with "B," then trace over a succession of dotted letters, signs of "real" language learning in preschool?

What you know, of course, is that nice, neat worksheets have no real meaning for a child who may dutifully complete them. Children need to manipulate real objects before they can talk or write about them. They need concrete experiences before they can understand and use objects symbolically in their language or play.

So what is important to remember and communicate to other adults is that children need a context for language.

They need to use it in response to their own interests, experiences, and needs. The child who struggles to write a "B" because he wants a sign for his "Bowling Alley" will have more understanding of that letter and sound than if he had traced it perfectly on a dozen worksheets.

Making language meaningful for young children means making it concrete and allowing it to evolve naturally. The suggestions below may be reminders. However, they are all ways of working with young children to enhance language as well as other areas of their development.

■ **Provide Hands-On Experiences.** Children need concrete materials to work with, but they also need lots of concrete experiences to expand their language and understanding of the world. Field trips that let children experience activities firsthand and handle "the tools of a trade," are a rich stimulus for language in all its forms. For example, during a visit to a car wash, arrange beforehand for children to help wash a car. Wet clothes can always be changed, but from this hands-on experience, you'll hear evidence of careful listening

as children imitate the sounds of the water-spray machine and descriptive words as they recall how the soap miraculously turned the dirty car clean. You may even see a sign for a "KWTR BKS" (quarter box) outside next to your trike-riders own car wash, or notice a new interest in stories about vehicles in your library corner.

■ **Encourage Idea Sharing.** A noisy room during play is a place where language is thriving! Idea sharing — between children, and between a child and yourself — helps to develop creative-thinking skills, fosters new concepts and communication skills, and often expands a child's vocabulary.

How can you encourage idea sharing? Ask questions! Make them thought-provoking and open-ended to encourage discussion: "What would you do if you saw a giant bean stalk growing in your yard?" "What do you think this pig puppet might say to this cow?" "How do you think we could get this boat to keep from sinking?" Avoid asking questions that have a "right" answer. Children may stop responding if they fear giving the wrong answer.

(continued on page 16)

Four-year-olds:

■ master most of the rules of language and use "adult-like" sentences.
■ love to talk and enjoy telling stories.
■ delight in shocking adults by using "forbidden" words.
■ create "different" voices for various roles in dramatic play.
■ enjoy stories about high-energy characters like themselves and books on subjects they're curious about.
■ are aware of words in their environment.
■ like to dictate words for an adult to record.
■ may begin to form some letters and try to write their name.
■ understand there is a connection between marks on a paper and their own movements; and develop eye-hand coordination that enables them to make lines, squares, rectangles, and circles.

Five-year-olds:

■ may use sentences that contain five or six words.
■ talk and talk — delighting in spontaneous conversations and in using "silly" words!
■ develop involved "scripts" during dramatic play and write labels and signs to enhance their activities.
■ have good control of writing implements and love to print and copy letters.
■ combine forms to create symbols in the pictorial or first-drawings stage.
■ describe their artwork and enjoy dictating stories about it or using invented spelling to write their own comments.
■ understand people can read words that are written down.
■ realize stories have a beginning, middle, and end.
■ appreciate books that are exciting but not scary, and ones with predictable rhymes that enable them to "read along." They also take pleasure in alphabet and number books.

HELPING CHILDREN GROW
LANGUAGE: THE SHORT COURSE!

Share this quick summary of key ways to help children develop listening, speaking, writing, and reading skills with aides, parent volunteers, and others in your program. Keep these tips handy as an occasional review for yourself, too.

HELPING CHILDREN LISTEN

• *Speak in a voice that helps children listen.* Try not to speak too fast or too softly. Give clear, simple explanations or directions. Use children's names to get their complete attention.

• *Model good listening skills.* Give children your full attention when they speak. Bend down so you make eye contact. Smile or nod to reinforce that you're listening. Be patient.

• *Help children understand why they are listening.* Point out why you want children to listen — to obtain information, as a courtesy, for enjoyment, etc.

• *Combine words and actions.* Talk about what you are doing so children can see and hear at the same time. For instance, while you're baking, explain your actions: "I am using a spoon to stir the dough."

• *Play listening games to develop sound awareness.* Listen to and guess sounds in your environment or imitate each other's silly sounds. (See the Activity Plans, pages 38-77, for listening games for all ages.) Keep listening activities brief, and end before children lose interest.

• *Listen to poems, chants, songs, and fingerplays, and read stories together every day.* Activities they enjoy motivate children to want to listen. Make stories, poems, and songs a part of the daily routine.

• *Provide a relaxed environment.* Clanging pipes or screaming fights hamper children's ability to concentrate on listening. Try to keep your atmosphere comfortable and relaxed. Quietly chatting in a cozy place is a wonderful way to learn about listening.

HELPING CHILDREN ARTICULATE

• *Provide experiences to expand verbal language.* Offer young children lots of objects to handle and name. Discuss actions and items during routines such as dressing. ("Here is your shirt. Let's button it.") Repeat fingerplays, nursery rhymes, and songs together. Encourage children to dramatize favorite stories.

• *Be a good speech model.* Use complete sentences when you speak. Offer children names for unfamiliar objects or new vocabulary related to a special interest. Extend children's own speech as you comment on what they're doing or saying. When a child says, "Sally, go," you respond, "Yes, Sally is going outside to play."

• *Be a good listener to encourage children to speak.* Show children that you're interested in what they're saying. Make eye contact and comment on their remarks.

• *Foster oral language through conversation.* Provide children with lots of opportunities to talk to each other individually, as well as in small or large groups. Encourage children to discuss their thoughts and feelings with you, too.

• *Ask open-ended questions to elicit verbal responses.* "What would happen if ...?" questions that allow for many possible responses encourage creative thinking and discussion. Try to avoid questions that require only a "yes" or "no" response.

• *Provide materials to promote speech development.* Well-chosen materials in every area of your environment will inspire lots of descriptive language and conversation.

Puppets encourage children to retell favorite stories or to make up their own. Dramatic-play props allow children to take on the roles and language of significant people in their lives. Sensory materials, like sand and water, encourage experimentation that leads to talk about what happened and why.

• *Play language games together.* Many time-honored games involve children in using words in imaginative ways. Young children enjoy saying "Pat-A-Cake" or singing "Ring Around the Rosie." Older children like to guess the answer to "I Spy With My Little Eye" or suggest favorite pizza toppings as they play Categories.

HELPING CHILDREN DEVELOP INTEREST IN WRITING

• *Let children see labels and see others writing labels.* Names on cubbies, brand names on cereal boxes, STOP signs — any kind of writing that has a function in children's lives encourages them to want to imitate and use these interesting marks.

• *Acknowledge children's first writing attempts — scribbles.* With encouragement and time, these scribblings will become lines as children gain control and understanding.

• *Offer children opportunities to experiment with a variety of media.* Finger paint, crayons, and modeling clay all help to improve eye-hand coordination and fine-motor skills that are necessary for writing.

• *Give children ongoing experiences with words and symbols.* Provide examples of everyday print in many forms — books, coupons, magazines, catalogs, etc. And give children materials to create print with — papers, markers, oaktag, paint — throughout your setting.

• *Arrange for experiences that lead to meaningful, integrated activities.* Children need reasons to participate in writing experiences that are meaningful to them. So, for instance, after a field trip to the airport, children might want to create an air-terminal center where the agent "writes" the tickets or makes a "schedule board" with flight information for passengers to read.

• *Encourage children to write often.* Involve children in writing thank-you notes, recipe charts, traffic signs, and stories about their own pictures. Applaud their efforts to experiment with writing words using "invented spelling" ("BLN" for "balloon").

• *Be ready when children need your assistance.* A child may ask how to print a letter or word or ask you to write out a story he or she wants to dictate. Your willingness to help and patience as children struggle with forming ideas and even letters are key to encouraging them to keep writing every day.

HELPING CHILDREN DEVELOP INTEREST IN READING

• *Expose children to books and more books.* For a first reading experience, an infant may sit in your lap while you point to pictures in a sturdy cardboard book. Toddlers like to turn the book pages and identify objects in the pictures. Preschoolers delight in stories that relate to their own experiences. Predictable books add to their active enjoyment as children chime in on repeating phrases or anticipated situations. Big books help children see the relationship between spoken and written words more easily. Wordless picture books encourage young children to tell their own stories.

• *Be a reading model for children.* Demonstrate the importance and usefulness of print. Read signs on the street and in the drug store during a neighborhood walk. Read the directions aloud while you make a snack together. Give children "junk" mail to look over while you read your mail. Show them how reading gives you pleasure as you share a book together.

• *Provide a print-rich environment that offers reasons to read.* Immerse children in print! Put grocery boxes and cans with labels in the housekeeping corner, along with a collection of coupons to read. Display posters of labeled buildings and cities in the block area. Hang recipe charts in the snack area.

• *Encourage children to use print to convey their ideas.* To help children eventually discriminate between scribbling, then letters, and finally words which have meaning, provide print-making materials such as paper and crayons, and ready-made "print" such as felt or magnetic letters. Encourage them to dictate stories or lists for group books or experience charts that everyone can try reading.

• *Extend children's reading experiences.* Allow lots of time to ask and answer questions about stories you share. Discuss characters' actions and emotions, and help children relate story plots and events to their own experiences. Encourage follow-up activities such as retelling a story in their own words with flannel-board characters, dramatizing it with puppets, writing a new ending, or just sharing the book again with a special friend. Motivate children to want to learn to read by helping them experience the joy of books and the value of words. Make sure books are always available — old favorites and new additions.

10 ALTERNATIVES TO LANGUAGE WORKSHEETS

The problem with using worksheets is that they usually ask for a specific right answer or imply that there's only one correct way to complete a task. They don't foster children's creativity or feelings of competence as capable learners.

To encourage creativity, divergent thinking, and self-confidence, offer open-ended activities that allow children to express themselves as individuals. Here are ten ideas to spark your own activity planning. Most are perfect for your library corner and writing center.

1 Invite children to cut or tear out pictures from magazines to paste on paper for category collages. Encourage themes such as colors or foods. *(reading)*

2 Play a classification game by inviting a child to use a marker to circle all the dogs or all the dolls in a magazine and to tell how they're alike and different. This is also a great activity for pairs to do together. *(reading, writing, listening, speaking)*

3 Turn paper towels into "movies" based on children's favorite stories. Provide children with several attached sheets of paper toweling and markers. Invite them to retell a favorite story, such as *The Three Billy Goats Gruff*, drawing a different story event in each paper "frame." Children can then roll up the pictures for showing and telling to an audience. *(reading, speaking, listening)*

4 Reproduce pictures from a favorite story and mount on sheets of oaktag. Cut each picture into several large pieces to create a story puzzle. Invite children to put the puzzles together, then to recall details from the stories. *(speaking)*

5 Alter familiar children's stories by creating new covers with new titles. You might do one for *The Four*

(continued from page 13)

Invite idea sharing by answering questions, too. Children are curious. They want to know why something happened or how a "D" looks. Think about their questions and give them your full attention. Be ready for questions that your answers may provoke!

■ **Follow the Child's Lead.** Meaningful language most often develops from children's own interests. Watch for those events that captivate children and build on them to enhance all forms of language. For example, you may notice a group of five-year-olds fascinated by a monarch butterfly on the playground. Sit with them and talk quietly as they observe its colors, note the rhythmic opening and closing of its wings, or watch it gracefully flutter away. Back inside, bring in written language by inviting the children to contribute their impressions to an experience story, recording their responses, then reading them aloud.

If children's interest holds, extend the experience further by reading an intriguing story such as *Where Does the Butterfly Go When It Rains?* by May Garelick (Young Scott). Pose that same question to children. Record their ideas — "It hides under its wings." "It flies under a mushroom." — on chart paper, to reinforce again the connection between spoken and written language.

An event that captures children's interest can become the theme for activities throughout your environment — from block corner to sandbox — especially for fives, who enjoy in-depth activities and projects that extend over several days or even weeks. For a personal example of one such event, see "Following Children's Lead Leads to Language!" on page 26.

■ **Involve Children With All Types of Print.** It bears repeating that saturating your environment with print is the most effective way to help children experience it naturally and develop an awareness of the function of written words. Offer magazines, newspapers, picture/word dictionaries, telephone books, colorful posters, birthday charts, and, of course, quality picture books. At the same time, be on the lookout for times during children's play when print materials might help to expand their activities and imaginations.

Invite children to contribute to the print in their environment by doing their own writing and by dictating to you. Pace your writing speed with their verbalizations — and be patient. Give children plenty of time to compose their ideas and change their minds.

When taking group dictation, it can be difficult for preschoolers to wait their turn to share a response. Lists are often easier to create in a group setting, such as "My Favorite Toy" or "Things to Take to the Beach," with each child's name written next to the shared idea.

Display individuals' dictated stories or group experience charts attractively at children's eye level, and encourage children to read and share their own work with others. Bind class or individual booklets and invite the authors to sign their books, too. When you display them in the library corner, you demonstrate to children (and to families) that their ideas are valued.

■ **Encourage Children to Take Risks With Writing** — Children's scribbles are their first attempts at writing. By applauding these marks, you encourage them to be risk takers and support their attempts at literacy.

Later, many young children try to write what they hear by using invented spelling. "MFN" might be a child's attempt to spell "Muffins," the dog in Margaret Wise Brown's *The Country Noisy Book* (Harper & Row). The sounds and marks may not be accurate, but they're an exciting beginning. After more experimentation, a child may write a full sentence such as "MFN Z A DG" — "Muffins is a dog."

Your encouragement and joy at this entrance into new forms of communication help motivate the child to continue experimenting with written language. Offer an array of materials to experiment with in your writing area and rotate the materials to keep it interesting and stimulating for children.

Books in your library corner can also introduce children to others, who, like themselves, are experimenting with written marks. After listening to *Harold and the Purple Crayon* by Crockett Johnson (Harper & Row), invite children to try out their own purple crayons on giant mural paper. On a wintry day, watch for children dragging a stick to make marks like Peter in *The Snowy Day* by Ezra Jack Keats (Viking).

SHARING BOOKS WITH CHILDREN

Books are at the very heart of your language program and deserve a special focus. Children can and should be read to very early, as soon as they're able to sit in an adult's lap. Snuggled closely, they learn to associate reading with enjoyment. Eventually, they will discover that there is information on the pages and that print and oral language are related in ways that have meaning.

And as you know, there is a multitude of books to read and enjoy together.

■ *Books for the very young* — There are wonderful beginning lap stories, such as *Buster's Morning* by Rod Campbell (Bodrick/Blackie), about a toddler who uncovers hidden objects and animals. For the very young, look for books that are simple, clear, and revolve around everyday events.

■ *Predictable books* — Good predictable books, as well as poems, nursery rhymes, songs, and fingerplays,

involve children by allowing them to anticipate what will happen through language patterns. Some predictable books are based on a sequence that helps children guess what will happen next. *The Very Hungry Caterpillar* by Eric Carle (Philomel Books), for example, eats its way through the week. By matching illustrations and text, books like *Goodnight Moon* by Margaret Wise Brown (Harper & Row) help children anticipate rhymes: "Goodnight kittens and goodnight mittens," "Goodnight bears and goodnight chairs." *Brown Bear, Brown Bear, What Do You See?* by Bill Martin Jr. (Henry Holt) brings children in with repetitive questions.

Many predictable books also lead naturally to dramatization. Generations of young children have built their own special bridge for the Three Billy Goats Gruff or have chased after the Gingerbread Man.

■ *"Big" books* — Enlarged versions of favorite stories, or "big books," enable children to see the text clearly while you read, helping them to become even more involved in the language process. Point to the words as you read, demonstrating the left-to-right progression of reading. At the same time, encourage children's comments. Watch children's joy in words and their sounds as they repeat silly-sounding terms or titles.

When they can see the text clearly, children often begin to recognize a particular written word in the context of what is happening or because it follows a story rhyme. *The Three Little Pigs* has "taught" countless children to recognize the rhyming phrase *huff and puff.*

The size of a big book makes it easy to share with a friend, and shared reading experiences assist young children in exploring and developing oral language. You can also provide a tape-recorded version of the story — one you purchase or create yourself — for children to listen to as they follow along in the book, expanding both listening and reading skills.

While many companies produce big books, you can make your own from

Little Pigs or *Goldilocks and the Three Monkeys.* (Draw silly pictures yourself or look for pictures to cut out and paste on paper covers.) Show children the covers and ask, "What if this happened in the story? What if there were four pigs instead of three? What if Goldilocks was in the house of three monkeys?" Encourage children to draw, tell, or write their responses and to create their own new stories. Remember to accept all ideas to keep stretching their imaginations. *(writing, speaking, reading)*

6 Record a portion of a familiar story, such as *Little Red Hen*, but stop before the ending. Invite a child to listen to the story, then to add his or her own ending on tape. Continue the fun by inviting other children to listen and add their own. Eventually gather all the "authors" to listen together to the story and their original endings. *(listening and speaking)*

7 Offer a variety of materials, such as modeling clay, yarn, and pipe cleaners, for children to create three-dimensional shapes and letters, or even words if they are interested. *(writing, reading)*

8 Provide trays of sand, salt, cornmeal, oatmeal, or shaving cream for children to practice making letterlike shapes, or, if they are interested, letters, numbers, or words. Or cut letters from sandpaper for children to trace with fingers. These sensory experiences will encourage lots of writing practice! *(writing, reading)*

9 Go for a walk and look at various license plates. Set out markers and cardboard rectangles the size of license plates. Invite children to design their own plates, including any shapes, designs, letters, or numbers they'd like. *(writing, reading)*

10 Plan an indoor or outdoor treasure hunt. Ask children to follow picture clue cards to find their way to a hidden treasure — a new book! *(reading)*

TIPS ON READING BOOKS ALOUD

▪ Preview a book before you read it aloud. Become familiar with the words so you can read smoothly and make eye contact with children. Think about open-ended questions you would like to ask to encourage discussions about the story.

▪ Gather props to enhance the story. You may have the perfect puppet for introducing the story, so be sure it's nearby when you're ready to read. Other useful props are stuffed animals and real objects that relate to story characters or theme.

▪ Eliminate possible distractions. Try to schedule your own storytime so that it doesn't coincide with distracting activities elsewhere, such as another group's playground time. Position children on the rug so they're facing you, not other temptations such as a cart of toys. Make sure everyone is comfortable. Hold the book to the side so that everyone can see the illustrations clearly.

▪ Preview the story with children. Start by naming the title and author and help children recall if they've met this character before in other books by this writer. Encourage children to try to guess from the title or picture on the cover what the book might be about.

▪ Be dramatic, be lively, have fun! Take on different voices for different characters. Use dramatic gestures. Encourage children to join in on predictable rhymes or to shout a warning to a character to WATCH OUT! Show that you're enjoying the story and help children to have fun, too.

standard-sized books by using an opaque projector to reproduce the illustrations. (Copyright laws allow you to make a single copy for personal use as long as you purchase the original book.) Hand print the text and laminate the pages so the book can withstand a lot of use.

Children also enjoy making their own big-book versions of favorite stories. Let them create their own illustrations, then dictate their words for you to write on each page. Be sure to laminate these pages, too, because children delight in reading their own books. And often, before long, they are truly reading them!

DEVELOPING LANGUAGE IN NON-ENGLISH-SPEAKING CHILDREN

When the children in your program represent many cultures, you may have some whose language at home is one other than English. Working with non-English-speaking children offers special challenges, but also special benefits, as all the children in your program are exposed to new cultures and languages and helped to understand and respect the exciting diversity of the world.

Your primary goal is first and foremost to insure that your non-English-speaking children feel accepted and valued in your program and comfortable with their own language. Your next objective is to gradually assist them with the process of learning standard English. Here are ways to help accomplish both goals.

▪ **Convey a positive attitude.** Be accepting of all of your children's cultural backgrounds and languages. Get to know their families and, if possible, how each family feels about language development. Support and encourage children's attempts at learning English. Be patient and model appropriate usage rather than correcting mispronounced words, so that children don't feel discouraged in their efforts to learn English.

▪ **Plan for cooperative activities among English and non-English-speaking children.** Involve children in simple projects, such as making play clay together or watering the plants. Help them get to know each other and find ways to communicate with each other in natural settings.

▪ **Offer role models for children's own language.** If you are not fluent in the languages of your children, enlist aides, volunteers from the community, or family members to work with the children in your room. These adults — who should also be English-speaking to allow for communication with you — can help create a more familiar and comfortable atmosphere, while offering children models for developing their native language.

Parents and other members of the children's ethnic community may also serve as resources for your whole group. They might share traditional stories with children, help them prepare traditional foods, or teach songs, dances, and games. (Be sure adults are comfortable with the idea before asking them to work with your whole group.)

▪ **Reflect diversity in your environment.** Label items around the room in the languages spoken by your children. Provide clothes, empty food containers, dolls, and other props in the housekeeping and dress-up corners that reflect all the cultures in your group. Make sure you display pictures that reflect the diversity of your group in non-stereotypical ways. Look for multilingual books, such as *Alphabet Times Four* by Ruth Brown (E.P. Dutton), which names pictures in four languages.

▪ **Make your daily activities multilingual.** Reflect the languages of your group. Count cookies for a snack in Navajo and in English. During water play, name objects that sink or float in Spanish and English. The bonus here is that all of your children — English- and non-English-speaking — will be learning a new language while refining their own!

CHOOSING BOOKS
FOR YOUR CHILDREN

Selecting just the right books for a group of children or for an individual child is an important step in providing a print-rich environment. Here are helpful tips on choosing children's books.

▼ **Consider children's interests.** What themes or characters intrigue your children most? Are books with rhyming words special favorites? Stay alert to children's interests and you'll select books they'll delight in. If there are particular authors children seem to enjoy, check *Children's Books in Print*, found in the reference section of most libraries, for more titles by those writers.

▼ **Consider your children's ages and developmental levels.** For babies and toddlers, books should be durable with simple, large, uncluttered pictures. Twos enjoy short, uncomplicated stories, while preschoolers like predictable stories, rhymes, and books that deal with feelings to which they can relate. Fives have a longer attention span and can follow a more involved story. For general guidance, books for younger children should take five to 10 minutes to read; books for older ones should take 10 to 15 minutes.

▼ **Consider the appropriateness of a story.** Children should be able to relate to the characters and plot. Avoid stories with characters or events that will be disturbing to children because of their age or own experiences. Look for stories that offer satisfying endings.

▼ **Review pictures and text to insure they are free of sex, race, age, and disability bias.** Are people of different cultures and racial and ethnic groups portrayed fairly, accurately, and authentically in the story line and through illustrations? Are the settings or environments of minorities described and illustrated in sensitive and positive ways? Are girls and women portrayed as active and successful? Do adult authority figures include women and minorities? Are the ability differences of people depicted in positive, mat-ter-of-fact ways? Are children spoken to and treated with respect? Are diverse family structures (single-parent families, biracial families, etc.), depicted in positive, non-stereotypical ways? Are there any subtle words, phrases, or ideas that may be demeaning or condescending? Any inferences or concepts that promote stereotypes? Can minority children identify positively with characters? Will the story broaden a child's understanding and knowledge of others? Will the book have a positive effect on children's self-esteem regarding their race, gender, ability, or culture?

▼ **Pay special attention to the pictures.** The illustrations will have the greatest impact on your non-readers, so be sure they are clear, colorful, and pleasing to the eye. The text should correspond closely to the illustrations, so children can follow the story from the pictures. If you will be using a book in a group setting, be sure the pictures can be seen clearly from 10 feet away. With younger children, it's often more successful to read a book twice to two small groups rather than to one big group.

▼ **Look for books that will involve children.** Are there rhymes to join in on or questions to answer? Look for stories children can dramatize or ones that will inspire them to make up their own ending, such as *Ask Mr. Bear* by Marjorie Flack (Macmillan).

▼ **Introduce children to classic tales.** Some stories are timeless and should be part of every child's early experience with literature. Look for fairy tales and folktales like *Sleeping Beauty*, *Goldilocks and the Three Bears*, and *Little Red Hen* in new releases with engaging illustrations.

▼ **Let children choose their own books, too!** Start children early in the habit of finding pleasure in a library. As soon as children can write their names, head for your public library to get library cards. Then, on frequent visits, help children make their own selections of books they'd like to hear.

SETTING THE STAGE
FOR LANGUAGE LEARNING

Everywhere you look there are labels and signs — a giant STOP in the block corner that children have helped to make; catalogs to cut up in the art center; magazines, phone books, and junk mail in the housekeeping area; and, of course, books, posters, and experience charts in the library corner and everywhere else: This is a print-rich language-learning environment.

When children are present, well-chosen materials and organized centers encourage listening and speaking. Interesting props inspire them to role-play, plan, and improvise. Conversation emanates from the sand and water areas as pouring and sifting lead to questions, predictions, and exciting discoveries. Puppets entice children to retell favorite stories, and the animal book shared at circle time naturally leads to imitating creature sounds and movements and to improvising new dialogue.

Setting up for language learning is a three-step process. It involves looking at your environment as a whole to insure that organization and atmosphere encourage language on a variety of levels; focusing on how language is used in each play setting and looking for ways to expand on that development; and creating centers such as a library corner and writing area that enhance and inspire reading, writing, listening, and speaking activities. This section will help you with each of these steps.

LANGUAGE, LANGUAGE, EVERYWHERE

In a child-centered setting, children are encouraged to make their own decisions about when to use language and what to do with it, so that language development occurs wherever children are found, in whatever they're doing, throughout every part of their day. Start your language check by looking at your environment as a whole. Use these points to help you evaluate how well the organization and atmosphere of your setting meet children's needs, let them take the lead, and stimulate all forms of language.

■ *Aesthetics* — Small details in your environment can have a big impact on encouraging language development. Colorful book posters in the library or donated store displays in the dramatic-play area are inviting forms of print. A bright quilt on the couch in the house-keeping corner encourages "mother" to read or sing to "baby." Attractive displays of children's art at their eye level encourage comments and discussion.

In general terms, an environment for young children is pleasing and interest-ing — a place where they want to play and learn. Shelves are well-organized and offer clear choices. Puppets, props, books, and blocks are of good quality and in good repair.

■ *Group Size* — You know that chil-dren need a daily routine that offers whole-group, small-group, one-on-one, and all-alone activities. These variations are important to enhance different kinds of language learning. Your setup signals activities that involve small-group inter-actions or whole-group sharing. For example, four chairs, spoons, and smocks in the snack area, along with a picture recipe chart and an adult with a sign-up sheet, prepare children to wait their turn for a small-group cooking project. A big circle suggests a large-group activity, such as moving to a jun-gle-sounds record after a trip to the zoo. A single rocking chair in the library reassures a child that it's just fine to sit peacefully all by himself or herself.

■ *Privacy vs. Open Space* — Most chil-dren need places to think quiet thoughts or share a secret with a friend. A large carton or bedspread thrown over a table makes a wonderful private retreat. As long as you have a clear view, a place on the floor behind a low cabinet works well, too.

■ *Concrete vs. Abstract* — Younger children need concrete objects to help them with conversations during play. For instance, a stove and refrigerator in the housekeeping area inspire a three-year-old to speak like a daddy baking cookies.

Older preschoolers generally need fewer concrete props. To them, the playground tunnel makes a wonderful rocket ship. However, they also need the potential for complex settings and materials to enhance language develop-ment, such as a hospital center complete with ambulances that come screeching into the emergency room and an operat-ing room with surgical "tools" and uni-forms to wear.

Occasionally these elaborate settings may encompass large areas of your room — such as the block corner becoming the operating room and the snack area turning into the hospital kitchen. Your flexibility allows play to develop where children's interests lead it — into listening, speaking, reading, and writing opportunities.

■ *Quiet vs. Active* — As you know, at any given moment the noise level in a room of preschoolers may vary from the shrieking sound effects of a chase on riding toys to the relative quiet of the art center or the sandbox. These variations are important. They are signals of a dif-ferent kind of language use.

Children need places where they can role-play a gruff giant barking orders to his golden goose or listen to the sounds that different instruments make. They also need quiet places where they can paint the flowers they saw on yester-day's walk or puzzle over why a mag-net picks up a paper clip but not a plas-tic comb. Your challenge in setting up is to make sure you allow for variations in noise and activity level — and that clanging musicians are as far away as possible from pondering scientists!

LANGUAGE DEVELOPMENT WITH MIXED AGES

The relaxed and cozy setting of a family day-care home offers many opportunities to develop all of your children's language skills.

■ Let each child try the same project in his or her own way. For example, to enhance writing skills, give each child a piece of dustless chalk to cre-ate with on the sidewalk. The baby's eyes can follow all the exciting markings others are making. Toddlers will scribble along, while preschoolers' marks will take on some form and may even look like letters. A five-year-old may choose to write letters and use invented spelling to form words, while school-aged children may write greetings to passersby.

Water applied with paintbrushes offers another kind of outdoor experi-ence that involves all ages.

■ Listening and language games involve all ages at once. For example, to develop listening skills, take turns hiding a ticking clock in another room. Together, walk through the room and listen to find its hiding place.

Provide a small plastic hand-held flashlight for each child (pair younger ones with older). Make the shining light go *up* to the ceiling, *down* to the floor, *under* the table, *out* the door. Tape colored cellophane over the light for new fun with color words. And if someone goes another way, that's fine, too.

■ When children "play house," offer pads of paper and markers for tak-ing phone messages. Gather a collec-tion of hats for children to put togeth-er an impromptu skit based on *Caps for Sale* by Esphyr Slobodkina (Addison-Wesley). Older children can take the speaking parts, while younger ones will have fun pan-tomiming the monkeys.

Collect items for a portable writing box. Use a plastic box with a cover and fill it with rubber stamps and stamp pads, markers, sheets of paper, pencils with erasers, and scrap paper of all kinds. You may want to help the youngest children choose items from the box, while older ones can learn to use it and clean up independently.

For quiet times, offer a book, a tape recorder, and an audiotape you have made of a story, so that one child or a pair can follow along on their own.

■ Invite older children to share books with younger ones or tell favorite stories. Preschool or kindergarten-aged children can "read" to infants and toddlers when they use a simple book with one picture per page, like *Dressing* by Helen Oxenbury (Simon & Schuster). When school-aged children share predictable stories, younger ones often chime in, such as with a loud or soft "trip-trap" for *The Three Billy Goats Gruff*.

■ When baking, use a picture recipe chart so that all of the children can read and help out. Later, when children are eating, ask, "How many different words can we use to describe these cookies?"

■ Promote awareness of language outside, too. Help build each child's awareness of language in natural ways. Read the signs and labels in the grocery store. Point out signs (STOP) and symbols (McDonald's golden arches) as you go along. Make a trip to the local library to check out books a part of your weekly routine.

■ Integrate language activities throughout the day. Point out words on the cereal box as you pour out breakfast. When you're diapering, sing songs and chants together. Use a child's sock as a silly hand puppet when you're dressing him or her after a nap. And enjoy those cuddly times when a child wants to sit on your lap to share a secret!

A SUPER SETUP

This illustration shows a library corner and writing center. (Situating these centers together enables children to have easy access to print samples as they write.) The numbers correspond with suggestions below.

1. Situate your library corner in a quiet, well-lit area. Place it by a window, if possible, to offer natural light.

2. Place an assortment of books, magazines, and children's dictated story booklets in a low, sturdy rack. Face covers out for ease of selection.

3. Add a rug to muffle noise. Provide soft, comfortable seating — big pillows, beanbag chairs — for enjoying books alone or with a friend.

4. Set up a listening area at a small table for listening to stories and songs on tape.

5. Store flannel-board characters and puppets on low, open shelves, for impromptu story dramatizations. More books can go here, too.

6. Add a high teacher storage shelf to serve both centers.

7. Use low shelves to organize print-making and manipulative materials in the writing center. Store in clear plastic boxes, with matching labels on shelves.

8. Display print samples, such as posters and chart lists, at children's eye level.

9. Offer other surfaces on which to compose, such as a chalkboard or magnetic board with letters.

10. Provide child-sized tables and chairs where children can write or draw.

11. Place the typewriter or computer by electrical outlets for safety and convenience.

HELPING LANGUAGE COME ALIVE IN EVERY PLAY SETTING

From this general look at your environment, focus on language development in specific play areas. Every area, as well as your playground outdoors, can engage children in listening, speaking, writing, and reading. While language development evolves naturally as children learn more about communicating their ideas, asking questions, and voicing objections during play, you can help. Use this review of key play areas to remind yourself of how children use language and how you can help enhance this use as they play.

■ **Housekeeping Center** — Oral communication is the stuff of which role-playing is made. Enhance it by providing an interesting assortment of props and letting children take the lead in developing their own play scenarios — deciding what characters they'll be and how those characters will act. Listen and observe their play to find out what other props you can add to further their interests and enthusiasm.

Encourage written language development by providing pads of paper and pencils for scribbling such things as shopping lists and telephone messages. Foster reading skills by offering print props such as telephone books, TV listings, and newspapers.

■ **Block Corner** — Listen in on your block builders and you'll hear language development as they plan how to create the bridge over the block road or discuss yet another way to get this tall tower to keep from collapsing! Make sure children have an assortment of accessory items — large and small vehicles, wooden and rubber animals, multiethnic figures, traffic signs, fabric, cardboard tubes, etc. — to encourage them to turn their block cities into play settings and to take on roles themselves.

Provide markers and posterboard in case children want to print store, traffic, and street signs; and chart paper for writing such things as a list of the hamburger toppings that are available in their newly constructed fast-food restaurant. If you pick up on particular interests, hang posters at their eye level. Skyscrapers and rocket ships offer additional forms of print, as well as construction ideas.

■ **Gross-Motor Area** — Large-muscle equipment, like the climbers and the rocking boat, often inspire adventuresome acts and imaginative dialogue. Look for props that can inspire new play themes and new avenues for language growth. For example, a simple blanket may turn a jungle gym into a camper's tent. A tape of wilderness sounds may inspire your campers to tell stories around the campfire — with an occasional peek over the shoulder, just to be sure those peeps, chirps, and growls aren't for real!

■ **Art Area** — When easels are available every day, children are inspired to paint, and then to find words to describe their creations. Offering children interesting accessories to use with modeling clay helps prompt conversations and dramatic play. For example, when candles are on the shelf near the clay, a cake and chorus of "Happy Birthday" may erupt!

■ **Science Center** — Exciting discoveries that encourage hands-on experimentation are a rich source of language. Providing an assortment of stimulating materials and plenty of time to explore, results in wonderful use of listening and speaking skills as children question, predict, and describe what they experience. Writing predictions on chart paper and displaying science-related books in that area enhance writing and reading skills as well.

■ **Sand and Water Area** — Limiting the number of children who can play at the sand or water tables to three or four helps further shared discussions and role-playing. Offering accessory items such as small boats or wheeled vehicles and plastic people may inspire dramatic

shipwrecks at sea or a pretend day at the beach. Containers of all shapes and sizes encourage lots of filling, pouring, and emptying, as well as the use of superlatives such as *heaviest* and *tallest*.

■ **Manipulatives Center** — Puzzles and other types of fine-motor materials in this area help refine the finger and hand muscles children use to write, as well as visual-discrimination and problem-solving skills. Math manipulatives such as attribute blocks, Cuisenaire rods, and colored wooden cubes encourage children to use oral language to explain or share the many ways they're discovering that they can classify, sort, match, order, compare, and count. Remember to stock paper and writing tools in this area to encourage children to write labels, numbers, or a "don't touch" sign for a puzzle in progress.

■ **Cooking Center** — Children get an array of print experiences when they "read" a picture-chart recipe, recognize the "orange" on the juice can, or dictate a favorite class recipe. Enhance speaking and listening skills by involving children in a discussion of the sequence of steps in making cookies or by naming as many red foods as they can.

■ **Circle Time** — All kinds of language development occurs here — listening to and saying fingerplays; hearing a song and interpreting it through dance; writing an experience story about the trip to the fire station; sharing a story, then talking about how a book character feels; or just talking — sharing thoughts, feelings, and ideas. Many activities you'll plan for in advance. But keep a stand with chart paper nearby so you're ready for spontaneous discussions that lead to group dictations of word lists or of predictions to check again later.

■ **Playground** — Of course, language development doesn't end indoors! Just watch children writing marks or crude letters in moist dirt or sand outside or listen in on the rich dialogue that develops as the climbing bars become a submerging submarine. With your help, a menu board appears for trike-riders at their "drive-through" restaurant. The excitement and freedom children feel on the playground helps to make it among the most inspired settings for language in your environment. Yet it's also the perfect place to be silent, for there are endless wondrous reasons to stop and listen — like a peeping baby robin or the quiet rustle of the wind stirring crisp autumn leaves.

CREATING SPECIAL PLACES FOR LANGUAGE LEARNING

While you want to integrate language into every area of your curriculum, into every nook and cranny of your space, you also need special places that are devoted to reading, writing, listening, and speaking — a library corner and a writing center. These areas complement each other and work well set up side by side. They are places where children know they'll find a book to cozy up with or paper and markers to create a sign for their shoe store.

THE WRITE STUFF

Looking for ideas to stock the writing center? Here's help with motivating children to write by offering lively and interesting materials.

■ Provide an assortment of writing implements: non-toxic marking pens, colored and lead pencils (primary and with erasers), ink pens, dustless chalk, and brushes and paint.

■ Vary the writing surfaces: chalkboard; envelopes and folders; tags; blank checks; and lined and unlined paper of different textures, sizes, shapes, and colors (such as index cards, construction paper, newsprint, old greeting cards, erasable slates, and ready-made blank booklets).

■ Add print makers: alphabet stamps and ink pads, magnetic alphabet letters, cookie-cutter letters and play clay, and a typewriter or computer.

■ Set out exciting accessories: child-safe scissors, tape, glue, paste, stamps, hole punch, stickers, ribbon, and yarn.

■ Display samples of print: signs, charts, advertisements, magazines, newspapers, pictionaries, and number and alphabet books.

Remember, too, that writing materials should not be restricted to the writing center. These same materials belong in other areas as well. So tuck a checkbook and pen in the housekeeping center for paying bills. Add cardboard rectangles and markers to the block corner for designing highway billboards. Place a blank booklet and marking pen in the snack area for recording favorite recipes. Follow the children's interests and preferences — and tap your own imagination — in stocking your room with "the write stuff"!

What should you consider in setting up both? The diagram on pages 22-23 offers a suggested organization to follow in developing your own blueprint. Here are some additional tips.

■ *Choosing a location* — A library corner and writing center are naturally quieter than the boisterous block corner or gross-motor area, so place them away from these noisier centers. Children will also need good lighting for reading and writing activities. A natural light source is best, so, if possible, locate the areas by a large window.

■ *Deciding on space size* — Naturally, the more space you can provide, the better. But unlike the block corner or dramatic-play area, where children need room to spread out, activities in the writing and reading areas take place at tables, in comfortable chairs, and on the floor. And besides, you want children to feel free to take a book to a newly constructed fort in the block corner or create a sign for their new store. It's far more important to stock these centers with materials that will entice children to want to visit them, even if the actual reading or writing ends up in another place in your room.

■ *Furnishings* — These should be inviting places where children can cuddle up with a book, sit comfortably and work on a story, or take some quiet time just to think. Your setup needs to accommodate children who want to work alone, those who want to look at a big book together, or those who want to dictate a story to you. Here are suggestions for furnishing each area in ways that encourage flexible and independent use.

▢ *Library corner* — This is the "soft" area of your room, so, if possible, you'll want a soft rug on the floor and giant pillows for stretching out with a book, as well as a small couch or big beanbag chairs for sharing a book with a friend. A rocking chair for enjoying a book alone or on your lap is a wonderful addition. A small table and chairs might serve as a listening area where children can sit alone or with a friend to hear tapes of stories and songs.

You'll also need low, open shelves for displaying books and storytelling props, such as puppets and flannel-board pieces that are kept in clear, labeled boxes. A cardboard theater for puppet performances and a folding flannel board should also find homes in

FOLLOWING CHILDREN'S LEAD
LEADS TO LANGUAGE!

Integrating language throughout your environment happens naturally when it comes from children's ideas and experiences. Here's an example from my own program — a serendipitous discovery that led to language and learning in nearly every area of our curriculum.

While on a walk one day, my preschoolers discovered a house being built. Their interest was so great that we decided to return to the site each day to watch the progress. We started an experience-chart diary to remember the changes in the house as it progressed, and some children drew pictures to hang in sequence beside the chart. We also brainstormed what we knew about building a house and listed our ideas on a chart, displaying it in our block center.

I located an old favorite, *Mike Mulligan and His Steam Shovel* by Virginia Burton (Houghton Mifflin),

your library corner. Colorful book posters — often obtainable free from publishers at conferences and bookstores — can add a touch of whimsy to the walls.

For tips on selecting books, see "Choosing Books for Your Children," page 19.

☐ *Writing area* — Comfortable and varied places to write are most important here. You'll need a child-sized table with several chairs so children can share and print written ideas or dictate their thoughts. If possible, provide a typewriter or computer and printer (on a secure table), which offer a different kind of writing experience. (Locate this equipment next to an electrical outlet so children won't trip over any cords.) A sturdy stand-alone chalkboard provides an interesting surface on which to compose, as does a felt or magnetic board with letter, number, and shape cutouts.

Low, open shelves are a must in this area to store print-making and drawing supplies, as well as individual samples of print, such as coupons, tickets, and greeting cards. Also put out materials to bind child-made books, such as a holepunch, colored yarn or brads, and child-safe scissors. (For additional materials to place in your writing center, see "The Write Stuff," page 25.)

To encourage independent use, store writing materials in clear, picture-labeled boxes, with matching labels on shelves, to aid cleanup. Smaller items can go in plastic, self-sealing bags, pierced several times for safety.

Clear bulletin boards and open wall space are important, too. You can display samples of print, language experience charts, as well as signs and advertising logos obtained from local merchants. These help guide and inspire your young writers as they work in the center. Children need space to display what they have created, too.

■ *Storage space for adult use* — As with any other area, you'll need adult storage space for extra supplies — paper and markers, materials not currently being offered to children, and supplies that don't belong in children's hands. Add a storage cabinet near the areas — or between them — to store special flannel-board pieces too delicate for everyday use or mat knives for turning a refrigerator carton into "The House That Jack Built"!

---

which we read while the basement was being dug. There was a lot of digging that week in the sandbox, too. Children explored measurement concepts and descriptive words, filling *big* and *heavy* buckets of sand and making *huge* holes. At the same time, our trucks were given special names such as "front loaders" and "backhoes." Children printed signs for the block area like the ones they saw at the construction site: DANGER! KEEP OUT!

As the house progressed, one child remembered *The Three Little Pigs*. We listened to the story, then created our own big book. The repetitive phrases enabled children to help read it aloud, and in no time they were dramatizing the pigs' plight, too. In the art area, children designed sculptures with straw, clay, and sticks, describing and comparing the textures using words like *hard*, *soft*, *prickly*, and *sharp*.

Fine- and gross-motor skills improved as every child built with saws, hammers, and drills. Some "wrote" labels for their structures, while others dictated stories to share. And children had fun singing the action song "Johnny Works With One Hammer" after their carpentry work was done.

When the real house was nearly finished, we built our own house with refrigerator cartons, decorating it with wallpaper on the inside and paint on the outside. As the culminating event, we wrote invitations to family members to come to our "Open House" for a snack. One parent even offered to share her copy of *The House That Jack Built*.

From a chance encounter on a walk, we experienced language in rich and meaningful ways. Children not only learned about language, but also made choices which gave them practice in decision-making skills, solved problems, and were creative in their own individual ways. It was an experience that we all learned from, still talk about, and will always remember!

— *Sue Miller*

LEARNING AND GROWING

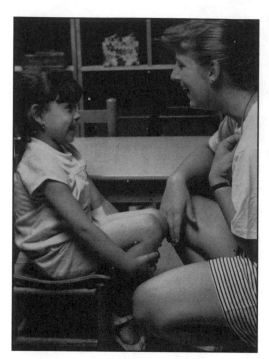

As a young child develops the ability to listen, speak, read, and write, a range of other skills and concepts are enhanced as well. Communication skills enable him or her to interact more fully with others and to express feelings more clearly. The world of books and written language encourages her to use motor skills and imagination to dramatize story characters or to write her own versions. And those are just the beginning of the ways that language aids in social, emotional, physical, cognitive, and creative development.

This four-page chart identifies some of the most important skills which language influences and which influence language. Share it with staff and families to enhance their understanding of the many dimensions of language learning.

Each entry begins with a description of how a key skill is supported by language. "Ways to Assist" helps you enhance development. "Developmental Considerations" reminds you of what to expect from younger (twos and threes) and older (fours and fives) children. Naturally, behaviors vary, so use these as guidelines only.

SOCIAL & EMOTIONAL DEV[ELOPMENT]

INTERACTION SKILLS

Language encourages and enhances social interaction. As children build together in the block area or pretend to be chefs in their own restaurant, they interact, exchanging props and plans and working out problems. Sharing books encourages dialogue, while discussing ideas for a group story exercises listening and other social skills such as cooperating and taking turns.

Ways to Assist
■ Organize your day so that children engage in many small-group and paired activities.
■ Ask questions to help start conversations between children or help them negotiate problems: "What else could you do to try to make the wheels turn?"
■ Provide children with experiences that give them something to talk about with each other! Offer books to look at, interesting props to play with, and field trips to places that will inspire dramatic play.

Developmental Considerations
■ Twos and threes often play by themselves or parallel to others — without interacting. Look for natural ways to foster interaction, such as cooking together.
■ Older threes, fours, and fives enjoy interacting through associative or cooperative play. Fives easily engage in spontaneous discussions.

WITH LANGUAGE

PERSPECTIVE-TAKING

As children role-play, they observe situations from a different point of view. *Little Red Riding Hood* offers three very different perspectives as children try out the roles of wolf, Red Riding Hood, and her grandmother. Children relate easily to many book characters, while others may challenge them to think about a situation in a new way. These explorations in perspective-taking often encourage empathy for others.

Ways to Assist
■ While reading stories together, encourage children to tell how they would feel or act if they were certain characters.
■ Help children explore feelings associated with roles they play: "Ambulance Driver, how do you feel when cars are in the way and you can't get your patient to the hospital quickly?"
■ Assist children in trying out roles that are new to them. A child who always plays the giant may benefit from gaining the perspective of "the little people."

Developmental Considerations
■ Younger children most often take the perspective of people familiar to them, such as a parent crooning to a baby.
■ Older children tend to speak and act like the characters they portray. They are usually aware that others may have points of view different from their own. They tend to be drawn to power roles.

EXPRESSING EMOTIONS

Language activities offer children natural outlets for expressing emotions. A story like *There's a Nightmare in My Closet* by Mercer Mayer (Dial Books) encourages children to discuss their bedtime fears. They may draw pictures and dictate stories about happy or confusing events and use pretend play to work through emotions, such as taking out feelings about new siblings on baby dolls.

Ways to Assist
■ Accept children's feelings. They need to know that anger and frustration are normal. Help them find appropriate ways to deal with these emotions.
■ Look for books and props that can help children work through strong emotions. For example, *Nobody Asked Me If I Wanted a Baby Sister* by Martha Alexander (Dial Books) may offer an opening for talking about a new baby.
■ Supply words for emotions that children can't express for themselves: "You are really angry with Steven for breaking your block house, aren't you?"

Developmental Considerations
■ Younger children usually lack the words to express how they feel, so they need help from you. When angry or frustrated, twos, who can't find the words, may bite or have a tantrum.
■ Older preschoolers tend to articulate their own feelings and portray emotions during role-play, such as being a frightened bunny, a crying baby, or a frightened Mama Bear.

AUTONOMY AND POSITIVE SELF-ESTEEM

Learning to speak, then to write, and eventually to read on their own gives children great feelings of independence and power. As they learn language in natural and meaningful ways and experience success, self-esteem blossoms, too. Feeling capable and confident is key to achieving success all through school and life.

Ways to Assist
■ Be open to children's ideas. Let them take the lead in making decisions about their own activities and play.
■ Set up your room to foster independence. Organize shelves so children can select materials and clean up on their own.
■ Create a warm and nurturing atmosphere where children feel accepted and where successes are acknowledged: "What a fabulous construction job!"
■ When children make mistakes, protect self-esteem by assuring them that it happens to everyone, and it's one way we learn!

Developmental Considerations
■ Younger children need simple, uncomplicated playthings to use successfully on their own.
■ Older children need to be able to make reasonable choices so they can try out their own decision-making and negotiating skills. Be alert to times when they need your encouragement to feel capable of going forward independently.

LEARNING AND GROWING

PHYSICAL DEVELOPMENT

MOTOR SKILLS

Language relates to motor skills as children use large muscles to dramatize and discuss being mountain climbers or fire fighters. When they draw pictures, scribble, and write letters and number formations, they use the fine muscles in hands and fingers.

Ways to Assist

■ Give children time and space to engage in dramatic play that involves gross-motor movements.
■ Read stories that inspire children to use gross-motor skills to dramatize the plots.
■ Enjoy action songs and circle games to help children associate words with movement. Offer many opportunities for children to explore movement in their own ways.
■ Provide interesting materials to engage children in art activities which help to refine small-muscle movements.
■ Furnish materials throughout the room so children can "write" in natural situations that are meaningful to them.

Developmental Considerations

■ Younger children like to imitate familiar actions and sounds. They need short, simple directions for songs and games. They also need to explore fine-motor materials knowing that it's okay to make a mess. Threes will start to show more wrist control.
■ Fours dramatize active characters, while fives' movement explorations are very involved. Both ages are gaining finger dexterity and like to try printing letters and numbers.

COGNITIVE DEVELOPMENT

VISUAL AWARENESS

A critical part of the language process occurs over time as children discriminate between scribblings, then letterlike forms, then letters, then words. With experience, this increasing visual awareness enables them to recognize letters in their names or to know if they're eating at Wendy's or Arby's. Through book sharing, children start to see that books are read from top to bottom and left to right.

Ways to Assist

■ Point out letters: "Look, you've written the 'M' in 'Mommy.'"
■ When children dictate a group story, point to the words as you read them. Help children find rhyming words (*huff/puff*).
■ Offer a print-rich environment so children have many samples to use, compare, contrast, match, and remember. Furnish writing tools so they can create their own print.
■ Offer letters and numbers that can be manipulated, like ones on a magnetic board, so children can observe and feel their similarities and differences.

Developmental Considerations

■ Younger children are still in the scribbling stage. Their eye-hand coordination is not refined enough to draw or recognize specific forms on request.
■ Most older fours and fives are beginning to form crude letters and enjoy trying to write their names. They may be able to read familiar forms and labels.

AUDITORY DISCRIMINATION

For children to eventually distinguish between letters or words, they need to discriminate between different sounds. Children are born with this basic ability. As infants, they can differentiate between their mother's or father's voice. Through practice, they refine this skill. When you read from the Helper Chart, it's exciting for Sara to discover that her name begins with the same sound as Serena's. Auditory memory also helps children recall the events in a story they enjoyed.

Ways to Assist

■ Ask children to pick out words that rhyme in songs, books, etc.
■ Play listening games that help children learn to discriminate between sounds: Clap a loud/soft pattern for children to imitate, or play a tape of familiar sounds and ask children to try to identify each one.
■ Observe auditory memory by asking children to mimic the sounds of familiar animals or objects.
■ As you share a book, focus on similarities and differences in the sounds of letters and words.

Developmental Considerations

■ Individual sounds are hard for younger children to distinguish. Play with sounds by imitating them and singing silly chants.
■ Let older children see printed words as you read to help them understand the relationship of letters and sounds. Encourage them to write words the way they sound using "invented" spelling.

WITH LANGUAGE

UNDERSTANDING SYMBOLS

Through language, children come to understand that symbols, such as an object or a mark, can represent something else. With experience, they recognize that written words are symbols that stand for spoken words. In the housekeeping corner, an older child will easily use a block to represent an iron as she sings, "This is the way we iron our clothes." When children use body motions to act out a song, they're representing events through symbolic gestures.

Ways to Assist
■ Supply print-making materials throughout the room for children to experiment with writing, drawing, and reading symbols.
■ Encourage children to use a pretend object when a real prop is not available. (With younger children, you may need to demonstrate how to use a block as an oar for the fishing boat.)
■ Incorporate familiar symbols into your environment. Boxes with the golden arches will turn your restaurant center into McDonald's in children's eyes.

Developmental Considerations
■ Younger children are very literal in their use of props. They relate best to real objects and often get ideas for play from them. They also need time to scribble with abandon.
■ Older children understand that letters, numbers, and words stand for something. They have more developed eye-hand coordination and may try writing these symbols.

PROBLEM-SOLVING SKILLS

Problems and conflicts are, of course, an inevitable part of life. As children's language skills improve, they gain an important way to articulate and solve their problems. As children listen to problems that book characters face, they're helped to see different approaches to problem solving and to examine effective and not-so-effective methods and solutions.

Ways to Assist
■ Help children learn the steps in solving a problem: Define the problem; talk about solutions; and select the best idea and try it. If it doesn't work, try another solution. Be very supportive of children's attempts.
■ Share stories with interesting predicaments. For instance, ask children what they would do if their home was filled with pasta, like the house in *Strega Nona* by Tomie dePaola (Prentice-Hall). Talk about how a character solves a problem and other ways children might solve it.

Developmental Considerations
■ Younger children need simple options to choose from when solving a problem. Support and expand upon their attempts at problem solving, too.
■ Older children will stick with a problem longer, but can become frustrated when several attempts to solve it don't work. Be there to help them keep trying.

CREATIVE-THINKING SKILLS

Creative thinking involves expressing and using language in new and challenging ways. As children dramatize roles in their own stories or create invitations to a dolls' tea party, they put their lively imaginations into words!

Ways to Assist
■ Ask open-ended questions that encourage children to explore many answers: "How would you like the story to end?"
■ Use a "magic wand" to grant powers or add props to encourage imaginative play: "You are now a king. Here is your crown."
■ Provide materials to extend creative thinking. With paper and a marker, a child can make a sign for "Fudgy Pizza Parlor."
■ Point out examples of creative thinking. For instance, discuss how clever *Swimmy* saves his friends in the story by Leo Lionni (Pantheon).

Developmental Considerations
■ Younger children's lack of verbal skills can make it difficult for them to put their ideas into words. Watch children's actions and point out examples of creative thinking. This age group prefers real props to pretend ones.
■ Older children have vivid imaginations, but usually need blocks of uninterrupted time to utilize their creative-thinking skills fully. Ask questions to challenge and extend their ideas.

ENCOURAGING LANGUAGE IN CHILDREN WITH SPECIAL NEEDS

QUICK TIPS & MATERIALS TO MAKE

Try these simple ideas to enhance language in children with particular handicapping conditions.

FOR HEARING-IMPAIRED CHILDREN

- When addressing the child, make sure you have his or her attention by saying his name or by touching him. Get eye contact before talking to the child.
- Talk slightly slower at a normal volume. Use gestures and facial expressions to clarify your words.
- Set up a special area where the child can listen with the tape recorder set at a higher volume.

FOR PHYSICALLY IMPAIRED CHILDREN

- Remove the paper from crayons. The warmth of a child's hand will help him or her maintain a firmer grip. A broken crayon provides a flatter, steadier surface to write with, too.
- Create huge markers the child can hold onto easily by filling clean roll-on deodorant bottles with tempera paint or colored water, then replacing the roll-on top. An empty shoe-polish bottle with a slanted foam-rubber top filled with paint also makes a steady writing tool.

FOR MENTALLY RETARDED CHILDREN

- Before you share a story with the whole group, read it to the child alone, or ask an aide or the child's parents to read it to him or her. Children with language delays benefit most from familiar stories, so they can follow the plot easily and recognize language patterns such as

---

Like other children, those with disabilities acquire language most easily in natural settings where speaking, listening, reading, and writing have purposes that are real to them. However, depending on the condition, learning language can be a complicated process for special-needs children.

On these two pages you'll find general tips and guidelines for enhancing language development in children with a range of abilities. The primary focus is on encouraging oral language, which children need most to be able to interact and socialize with other children and to feel accepted and "normal." Remember, though, that specific methods for helping a child develop oral and written language skills are best decided on in consultation with the child's therapist and parents.

HOW DISABILITIES AFFECT LANGUAGE DEVELOPMENT

Particular conditions impact language learning differently.

- *Hearing-impaired children* need lots of help with listening and speaking. Because they can't hear language well to help them model it, their oral-communication skills are often greatly impaired.

- *Visually impaired children* may not be able to read and write in a conventional way. They may have a more limited speaking vocabulary because their range of experiences is more narrow. However, their listening skills can be quite acute.

- *Physically impaired children* may have difficulty speaking because of a head or neck brace or other kind of equipment. Impaired motor skills may affect the child's ability to develop writing skills at a normal pace.

- *Mentally retarded children* lag behind their same-aged peers in development, so a child's speech, listening, reading, and writing skills are often consistent with a much younger child.

- *Children with behavior disturbances* often have difficulty using and refining language skills in natural ways. A withdrawn child may not talk with others, an aggressive child may alienate play partners, while a hyperactive child may not be able to sit through a story or listen without being distracted.

HOW YOU CAN HELP

There's much you can do in general and specific ways to encourage language development in special-needs children. Here are suggestions to try.

- *Encourage children to engage in language-rich activities.* Children with disabilities tend to interact with peers less often, and they miss out on using conversational skills. To help a special-needs child engage in dramatic play, for example, encourage him or her to explore the play area and become familiar with it. Give her time to examine objects in the area. Talk about how different objects, such as cooking props, might be used in different roles. Play with the child to guide her in taking on a role. When other children are in the area, observe play and look for ways

peating favorite rhymes and songs helps a child recognize language patterns such as rhyming words. Children also benefit from the confidence that comes with mastering the words in a story or song.

she can be included, such as by taking the role she practiced with you.

■ *Help children to encourage responses from others.* Special-needs children sometimes speak with little facial expression or animation in their voices, and so are less likely to invite responses from others. Help a child use gestures, like a smile when saying "hi," that tell others she wants to interact.

Encourage other children to talk to a special-needs child and to respond to her words: "Sara wants to know about your rocket. Tell her about it." When the special-needs child responds slowly or talks unclearly, you may need to act as interpreter — without making the child feel self-conscious, of course — to keep a dialogue going.

■ *Model lots of language.* Narrate the child's actions: "You're digging in the sand. You made a big hole with the shovel." Talk with the child about what you are doing. For example, if you're tying her shoe, describe each step.

■ *Give words meaning.* Use concrete experiences to help a special-needs child learn words for objects and concepts. (This is especially important for mentally retarded children.) *Clean* has more meaning when a child helps clean up after snack, washes toys in the play area, and washes her own hands. It's easier to learn *soft* if the child is touching a soft pillow than listening to someone say, "A pillow is soft."

■ *Share stories, songs, and fingerplays to encourage fun with language.* Re-

■ *Set up situations where the child needs to use language.* For example, you might ask a child to deliver a message to another adult in the room: "Please ask Karen to get the tape recorder." Note daily situations that prompt her to talk with others or to try out written language, such as during outdoor play, storytime, or dramatic play. Try to arrange her day so she can spend more time at these activities.

■ *Respond to a child's words in a positive way, while encouraging more complex language skills.* If a child says, "Play ball," expand on the statement with, "I want to play ball, too." When a child says, "I felled down," echo the words, not correcting her but using correct grammar: "You fell down! Are you okay?" When a child omits a word, repeat the sentence, emphasizing the missing word: "Did you say you want *the* ball?" But don't expect the child to repeat the statement after you.

■ *Help all children understand that there are many kinds of language.* Teach your group to use sign language to communicate with a hearing-impaired peer. Contact your local society for the blind about borrowing a Braille typewriter for children to see the system of raised dots which some visually impaired people read. Look for ways to enhance children's understanding of language and of their special peers.

Information and ideas contributed by Merle Karnes, Ed.D., professor of special education, University of Illinois, Urbana; and Susan Miller, Ed.D.

rhymes or predicable elements. Repeat a child's most favorite stories frequently.

FOR VISUALLY IMPAIRED CHILDREN

■ **Read aloud** stories that have a strong plot to keep the child's interest. Share books with raised surfaces and interesting textures which the child can feel.

■ **After listening** to a story such as *Little Red Riding Hood*, offer the child pre-cut shapes of the wolf, Red Riding Hood, Grandma, and other characters to feel, then to paste onto paper. Encourage the child to dictate a retelling or other reaction to the story.

■ **Help the child** learn letter and number shapes by feeling sandpaper cutouts or magnetic letters. You might guide a child's hand as you write letters or numbers in the air, so the child feels the motions involved in forming letters or numerals. Look for toy blocks with raised letters for a child to feel.

FOR CHILDREN WITH BEHAVIOR DISTURBANCES

■ **Children** whose behavior is hyperactive or aggressive need lots of structure at storytime. Keep stories short to match attention spans. Seat the child near you, and be sure there are no distractions such as a toy he or she has brought with her or a box of blocks nearby.

■ **When creating** a group list or responses to a story, have a child with a short attention span go first, to involve the child, yet free her to move on to other activities.

■ **A withdrawn** child may be helped to use language and feel more secure by speaking through a puppet.

TALKING WITH FAMILIES ABOUT LANGUAGE

Many parents think of learning about language and remember worksheets, desks, and basal readers. You may need to help them understand that language — listening, speaking, writing, and reading — becomes meaningful to children through play experiences, through acting out imaginative roles, labeling block structures, manipulating marking items in wet sand, and choosing their own books. You can also help them see that their child develops socially, emotionally, physically, and cognitively as he or she interacts with others in an exciting hands-on integrated environment.

Here are ways to communicate to families that an open, print-rich environment is not only fun, but it is also a developmentally appropriate way for their children to learn language.

■ *Program visits* — Before a child enters your program, explain how language and play are interrelated. Encourage questions and invite parents to relax in the book corner, read dictated stories, and notice how materials and storage places are labeled. Also, encourage parents to visit often to observe dramatic play and children using the writing center materials, and, if possible, to become volunteer readers and writers.

■ *Parent space* — Display language-related activities families can participate in, such as directions for making a puppet. Provide books and articles on language topics.

■ *Drop-off and pick-up conversations* — As parents arrive, share and personalize their children's language development. "Jan was a teller in the bank this morning. I wish you could have seen all the numbers she wrote on the deposit slips!"

■ *Parent workshops* — Talk about how children learn through play. Put out samples of their dictated stories as well as high-quality published children's books. You might even do a little role-playing so parents better understand appropriate techniques for encouraging — without interfering with — play. Encourage family members to relate their feelings and ask questions.

■ *Newsletters* — Send home practical ideas — listening games for the car pool or samples of fingerplays. Include samples of children's writing.

■ *Videos* — Parents and family members might enjoy a videotaped session of the children's day with a short overview explaining some of the language activities they will see. (Make sure you have signed release forms for every child in the video.)

■ *Books* — Encourage children to take home class books and big books they have created to share at home.

■ *Parent conferences* — This is a wonderful one-on-one time to talk about children's involvement with language and share their achievements through anecdotes.

■ *Telephone calls* — Make these positive events, letting your language and tone convey your excitement about children's ability.

■ *Notes* — Send a short, sunny note home to let everyone know that Sandi began to write her name today or Jeremiah dictated an entire page of riddles. And be sure to send home a copy of the parent letter on the right, too!

SHARING LANGUAGE FUN AT HOME!

Dear Family,

When you responded to your child's first cries, you immediately became involved in encouraging your child's language skills. Your child still needs your support and acceptance as he or she gets older and tries out new language ideas. Here are some suggestions to try together.

1. *Read books together every day.* Ask your child "what would happen if ..." questions about the stories. Encourage him or her to share predictions and personal reactions. Help your child take out books with his or her own library card. Have fun with rhyming words — in fact, just have fun!

2. *Create your own books.* Write down stories your child dictates about his or her artwork or a trip you took together to the dentist. Encourage your child when he or she is ready to write the words in the story the way they sound, using "invented" spelling. Punch holes in the pages and tie yarn or ribbon to hold them together to form a book.

3. *Play language games.* Together, make up a "picture" shopping list with can and box labels. Match this list with the items in the store or try saying as many words as you can that rhyme with cat.

4. *Make a writing box.* Gather items to "practice" writing — markers, crayons, pencils, erasable slates, index cards, lined paper, envelopes, and colored paper. Keep it near where you write your bills or letters so you can write together.

5. *Arrange a "prop" basket.* Use scarves, old shoes, hats, etc., to act out stories and pretend to be people in the neighborhood or imaginary creatures. Encourage conversation and supply words or a prop to help extend the play. "Here's the phone (a shoebox) to call the police!"

6. *Sing songs.* Let your child teach you songs, or make up your own words to familiar tunes, such as "Mary Had a Little Lamb."

7. *Gather collections.* To help your child notice and talk about similarities and differences (important to note when learning to read words), collect large buttons, colorful lids, and swatches of different-textured materials. Talk about color, size, shape, or texture (just one at a time)! Make comparisons — bigger, smoothest, rounder, softer, etc.

Please let us know some of your family's favorite language ideas so we can share them on our Parent Bulletin Board.

Sincerely,

_____

Teacher

USING THE
ACTIVITY PLANS

Use these plans to offer experiences — both familiar and new — that will enhance language and other kinds of skills. But use them for more, as well. Use the listening games as models for developing your own listening activities. Use the art suggestions to increase your own awareness of how to expand expressive language through creative expression. Use the tips on sharing stories to expand your own use of children's books. Let these plans support you in developing your own abilities to enhance language in everything your children do.

GETTING THE MOST FROM THE ACTIVITY PLANS

Because each plan is designed with a specific age in mind, the set together offers help in structuring language experiences that are developmentally appropriate to the interests and abilities of twos, threes, fours, and fives. Naturally, these ages represent a wide range of developmental levels, so you may find that certain plans need to be adapted for your particular group. And to truly get the most from the plans, look at all 40 for ideas to simplify, modify, or extend for your children.

The format is simple and easy to follow. Each plan includes most of these sections:

■ *Aim*: The value of the activity is explained through a list of language skills that are developed most fully — listening, speaking, reading, or writing — as well as other skills or concepts that are enhanced.

■ *Group Size*: The suggested group size is the optimum number of children to involve at one time. Naturally, you should adjust this number to meet your own needs.

■ *Materials*: Basic materials — most of which you'll already have in your room — or special items to gather are suggested here.

■ *In Advance*: This is an occasional heading found in some plans. It often outlines materials to prepare or arrangements to make before introducing an activity.

■ *Getting Ready*: Here you'll find ways to introduce the theme to one child, a small group, or a large group at circle time. Open-ended questions help children think about a topic. Handling props, brainstorming ideas, creating experience charts, and sharing stories are other ways to encourage involvement and language skills.

■ *Begin*: Let the activity begin and the language flow! Here you'll find suggestions for introducing materials; for helping children get started; or in the case of circle games or fingerplays, words and actions to enjoy with the children. As well, you'll often find more open-ended questions to stimulate language and play. Some activities feature extension ideas to further enhance an experience.

■ *Remember*: This section offers developmental considerations to keep in mind about how children develop language and what to expect from different ages. There may also be an occasional safety reminder or a tip on ways to relate other skills and concepts to the activity theme.

■ *Books*: The books at the bottom of each page are a beginning selection of what's available to fit with each theme. Share them as part of the activity, or add them to your library corner for independent enjoyment.

SHARING THE PLANS WITH OTHERS

Let these plans serve as resources for others, too, by making them available to assistant teachers, to aides and volunteers, and to family members. (You may duplicate each activity page for educational use.)

When you share these plans, you communicate your philosophy of child-centered learning. By offering ideas on how to present language in a natural way, you help other adults in children's lives to remember that language is a part of every activity in which children engage — and that making language meaningful for children is what helps them to learn language and to find pleasure in its use.

USING THE ACTIVITY INDEX

The index on pages 78-79 lists each activity plan, along with the developmental areas and skills it enhances. Use the index to:

▼ Determine the full range of skills and concepts covered in the plans.

▼ Highlight specific skills or developmental areas a plan reinforces when talking with family members.

▼ Identify and locate an activity that reinforces a particular language skill on which you want to focus.

▼ Assist in finding activities that complement your group's present interests.

ACTIVITY PLANS

FOR TWOS, THREES, FOURS, AND FIVES

LANGUAGE

Think about, talk about, and have fun acting out ...

TAKING CARE OF ME

Aim: Children will use listening and speaking skills as they role-play familiar household routines.
Group size: One to four children.
Materials: Simple, unbreakable, familiar items from the dramatic-play area, such as household and kitchen items and empty food containers; dolls and accessories; and dress-up clothing.

GETTING READY

You can build on the familiarity of household routines to expand twos' language skills. Observe as your children play with the various objects in the housekeeping area. Watch for opportunities when you can join one or two children to engage them in conversation without disrupting their play.

BEGIN

Play alongside children for a while. Speaking aloud, explain that you are pretending this is your house, and review who lives in your house with you. As children show interest in what you are doing and saying, invite them to pretend that the housekeeping area is their house, too, and ask them to talk about who lives with them. Listen carefully to each child's response. Some children may talk about Daddy, Grandma, or "Milly," who might be a neighbor, baby-sitter, or pet. Then ask, "When Mommy (or Daddy or Milly) takes care of you, what does she do?" If this general question does not spark a response, follow up with a more specific one such as, "Who fixes food for you to eat?" If one child has been playing with kitchen items, you might ask, "Are you a mommy (or daddy) fixing food? What are you making?" Wait for the child's response, then ask another question such as, "Who are you cooking for?"

Lots of Language Over Time

Use household-play props to encourage twos to talk about everyday routines in their homes whenever it's natural. For example, you might ask a child who is washing dishes in the housekeeping area or at the water table, "Who washes dishes at your house? Do you ever help?" Encourage children to show and tell you how Grandma sings the baby to sleep or how Daddy sets the table. Watch for other kinds of role-playing by children to lead into discussions of buying groceries or cleaning around the house.

Remember

▪ Many twos have limited language skills. First and foremost, be patient. Listen to the child's responses, and model language by expanding one- or two-word answers into complete sentences.
▪ Encourage early forms of writing by providing paper and markers for twos to use. Model meaningful written language by offering to write a grocery list for a child who's "going shopping" or a note for "Daddy" to tack to the play refrigerator. Some twos will want to do their own writing, too.
▪ Always positively acknowledge that in each family structure, there is someone who cares for each child.
▪ Try to provide dolls, food, and clothing that are representative of the cultures of your children.

BOOKS

| Enjoy these books about all kinds of families. | ▪ *Brothers and Sisters,* edited by Debby Flier (Checkerboard Press) | ▪ *Grandpa and Me* by Neil Ricklen (Simon & Schuster) | ▪ *Teddy and Me Pretend to Be* by M. Rogers (Brimax Books Limited) |

a b c LANGUAGE

Here's another familiar experience that will inspire descriptive language from twos.

LET'S GO FOR A RIDE!

Aim: Children will use listening, speaking, and motor skills as they role-play riding in a vehicle.

Group size: Two or three children.

Materials: Dolls, small chairs or hollow blocks to sit on, a child's car seat, and a few play or real steering wheels. (If you can locate an old car seat with seat belts attached, bring it in!)

GETTING READY

Place the car props in the block or dramatic-play area. When you notice a child or group of children taking interest in the steering wheel, car seat, and other items, join the group. Ask, "Where have you seen these before? What do you do with them?" Be patient and give children lots of time to share riding-in-the-car experiences.

BEGIN

Let children play with the car props in their own ways. They may enjoy pretending to drive themselves or might put a doll in the car seat to take to the doctor. Listen for the kinds of talk and sound effects — car motors and horns, for example — that evolve spontaneously from this type of meaningful activity.

At moments when you won't be interrupting play, ask questions to expand language skills: "Are you a mommy driving your baby? Where are you going today?"

Sing a Song

Introduce the song "Wheels on the Bus" as children play. Try changing the words to mirror individual children's play. For example, if Jacob is pretending to drive a bus, you might sing:

Jacob's on the bus and driving around,
Driving around,
Driving around.
Jacob's on the bus and driving around,
All around the town.

Remember

▪ Twos are just developing language. Often you may get a one-word answer or a very simple sentence — "Mommy take me." — in response to a question. Encourage and extend twos' language by restating replies: "That's right, Meredith. Mommy brought you in the car."

BOOKS

| Here are delightful books about things to ride in. | ▪ *Mr. Little's Noisy Truck* by Richard Fowler (Grosset & Dunlap) | ▪ *Wheels on the Bus* by Raffi (Crown) | ▪ *When I Ride in the Car* by Dorothy Chlad (Children's Press) |

a b c LANGUAGE

Words and actions are the perfect combination.

HAVING FUN WITH LANGUAGE

Aim: Children will use listening, speaking, and gross-motor skills as they act out simple verses.
Group size: Individual children, small groups, or whole group.
Materials: None.

GETTING READY

Choose a simple action rhyme or fingerplay — just four to six lines long — and memorize the words and actions. Here are three rhymes that are great for two-year-olds.

Tell Me, Do
Tell me, tell me, tell me, do.
Tell me, tell me, who are you?
(Adult looks at a child).
Let's roll the ball and find out who.
(Adult rolls a ball to a child.)
What, oh, what's your name?
(Child with ball answers his or her name.)

Jack-in-the-Box
Jack-in-the-Box
(Make a fist with thumb stuck inside fingers.)
Sits so still.
Why don't you come out?
I think I will.
(Spring thumb out from under fingers while making a popping sound with your lips.)

Elevator Ride
Elevator ride, elevator ride,
We go up, high as the sky.
(Children's voices go higher as they raise arms up.)
Elevator ride, elevator ride,
We go down, low down, and hide.
(Children's voices deepen as they squat down and hide their faces under their arms.)

BEGIN

Make eye contact with one or two children and begin to recite a rhyme. Speak slowly, pronouncing each word clearly so that children can understand and imitate you. Use lots of facial expressions and exaggerated movements. Children will join in as they feel comfortable. Try repeating the rhyme often throughout the day.

Remember

▪ Toddlers often understand many words before they use them. Their vocabulary grows by hearing others use a variety of simple words and phrases over and over again during the course of a day.
▪ Extend children's two-word phrases into sentences. For example, extend "red ball" into "Nicholas has a red ball."

BOOKS

| These books offer more rhymes, songs, fingerplays — and words — for twos. | ▪ *Baby Games* by Elaine Martin (Running Press) | ▪ *Look at Me: Activities for Babies and Toddlers* by Carolyn Buhai Haas (CBH Publishing, Inc.) | ▪ *Music for Ones and Twos* by Tom Glazer (Doubleday) |

LANGUAGE

These fingerplays and rhymes will keep your twos singing!

FINGER PUPPETS AND FINGERPLAYS

Aim: Children will experience the rhyme and rhythm of language and use listening, speaking, and motor skills.
Group size: Whole group.
Materials: Non-toxic, water-based marking pen.

GETTING READY

Gather children in a circle. Begin by singing a few songs or chanting some fingerplays your twos already know, such as "Hickory, Dickory Dock," "Jack and Jill," and "Baa Baa Black Sheep." As children sing, demonstrate simple hand movements or clap to act out each rhyme.

BEGIN

Before you share more fingerplays, use a pen to draw a simple face (two dots for eyes and a curved line for a smile) on each of your index fingers. As you begin the following chants, let these two fingers have a "conversation" or sing each other the following song. Children will enjoy this and may begin to imitate your actions. Some will want faces on their fingers, too.

These Are My Eyes
Each child will need a partner for this fingerplay.

These are my eyes.
(Point to eyes.)
This is my nose.
(Touch nose.)
These are my fingers.
(Hold up fingers and wiggle them.)
That tickle your toes!
(Partners tickle each other's toes.)

The Pointing Chant

We point to the ceiling.
(Point to the ceiling.)
We point to the floor.
(Point to the floor.)
We wave to each other.
(Wave to others.)
And walk out the door.
(Everyone walks out the door —
then walks back in!)

Remember
▪ Don't expect your twos to follow along perfectly. They'll enjoy the rhyme and rhythm of the language and the sharing together, which is what's most important.
▪ Puppets are a wonderful way to encourage children to use language, especially shy ones who may be more comfortable speaking through a puppet. Stock your center with a range of puppets, from commercially made ones to characters made from gloves, socks, and old mittens. Check puppets frequently to be sure sewn-on features are securely in place.

BOOKS
Here are books with other good ideas for fingerplays and puppet fun.

▪ *Creative Teaching With Puppets* by B. Rountree, M. Shuptrine, J. Gordon, and N. Taylor (The Learning Tree)

▪ *Move Over, Mother Goose* by Ruth I. Dowell (Gryphon House)

▪ *One Potato, Two Potato, Three Potato, Four*, compiled by Mary Lou Colgin (Gryphon House)

a b c | LANGUAGE

A natural conversation is the best way to enhance language skills.

WHAT'S OUTSIDE OUR WINDOW?

Aim: Children will use listening and speaking skills, then experience their words in print.
Group size: One to six children.
Materials: Chart paper and marker.

GETTING READY

When children are inside, what's happening outside can be a source of endless fascination. Let this activity build on what you see children doing spontaneously. For example, you may be holding a child on your lap near a window and talking together about what you see outdoors. Or you may be observing one or several children who are intrigued by something outside.

BEGIN

Use this moment to engage children in a conversation that helps to develop language and models good listening. Listen to the words children use to describe what they see. Help them expand their language skills by restating what they say in a complete sentence: "Travis sees a lady in a blue hat walking by," or "Adam sees a fat gray squirrel climbing up a tree." Expand on children's language and thinking skills by asking them to make simple predictions: "Travis, where do you think the lady in the blue hat is going?" or "Adam, what do think that fat gray squirrel will do next?"

Write a List of What You Saw

When the people or creatures disappear from view and twos begin to lose interest, invite them to make a list of all the things they saw outside. Write their words on chart paper, adding the child's name and a simple picture symbol for each word, such as a stick tree next to the word *tree*. Review the list with children, marveling at all the things they saw and remembered. Display the chart where family members can see and comment on it.

Read a Story, Too

Another wonderful follow-up to your conversation is sharing a story together about being outside or, better yet, looking out from inside, as the children have done. The list below offers some good stories to consider. Be sure each child can see the pictures clearly as you read. Talk about the pictures in the book and whether any look like scenes the children can see from their windows.

Remember

▪ Children will have much more to say if you build on their natural curiosity. Don't force the sharing. Wait until you see children engrossed in something outside.

BOOKS

| Look together at these books about looking outside. | ▪ *Brown Bear, Brown Bear, What Do You See?* by Bill Martin Jr. (Henry Holt) | ▪ *Nature Walk* by Douglas Florian (Greenwillow Books) | ▪ *Night Cars* by Teddy Gam (Orchard Books) |

a b c LANGUAGE

Let pictures of your twos encourage a thousand words!

WHO IS THIS?

Aim: Children will use listening, speaking, and observation skills to identify familiar faces.

Group size: Two to four children.

Materials: Photos of each child in the class and an instant camera (optional).

In Advance: Ask family members to bring in a photograph of each child, one that clearly shows the child's face. Bring in a photo of yourself as well. Place all photographs in a shoebox.

GETTING READY

This is a good activity to introduce with a group of children who are restless and not engaged in regular play options. Young children enjoy looking at photographs, especially of themselves. This activity can help them focus and encourage their talking!

BEGIN

Share the photographs of just the children in your small circle. As you show each one, talk about it. Ask, "Who's this? That's right. That's Carly! Carly, what are you doing in this picture? Who is in the photo with you? Yes, that's your mommy! What is Mommy doing? What do you and Mommy (or Daddy, Grandma, etc.) like to do together?"

Our Day — In Pictures

If you have access to an instant camera, take pictures of children involved in various activities during the day. Twos will love watching the photos develop right before their eyes! Can they guess who is in the picture as it becomes clearer and clearer?

Put the photos together in an album. Let children help you choose the words to use in labeling each picture. Place the photo album in your library corner where children can look at it on their own. Occasionally review the photos with one or two children, listening as they look and talk about what they see. Add more pictures to it throughout the year. You'll find the photos will spark not only language but fond memories, too!

Remember

- Be sure to include a photo of each child in your album.
- Select a durable album of the type that lets you insert the pictures behind clear plastic, so that the photos are protected from little hands.
- Display your photo album for families to look through and enjoy. It helps them to see at a glance what kinds of activities their children are doing.

BOOKS

Help your twos learn more about themselves and the world around them with these stories.

- *I Go to Sleep* by Margery Facklam (Little, Brown)

- *I'll Try* by Karen Erickson and Maureen Roffey (Viking Kestrel)

- *I Spy: Picture Book of Objects in a Child's World* by Lucille Ogle and Tina Thoburn (American Heritage)

LANGUAGE

Cooking together is such a language-rich activity.

MAKING APPLESAUCE

Aim: Children will use listening and speaking skills and all of their senses as they help make applesauce.

Group size: Three or four children.

Materials: About 12 baking apples; two basins, vegetable scrub brushes, dishcloths, plastic bowl, paring knife, saucepan, and wooden spoons; cinnamon and lemon; and paper cups, plastic spoons, and napkins.

GETTING READY

Let children handle the apples. Help twos find words to describe how they look, such as *round*, *red*, and *shiny*; how they feel, such as *smooth* with a *hard* stem; and how they smell, such as *sweet*. Peel and slice one apple and give a wedge to each child.

(Put the knife out of children's reach immediately.) Encourage twos to describe how the apple tastes, such as *yummy!*

Now put out the basins filled with cool water, the vegetable brushes, and the dishcloths. Invite twos to help you wash the apples, then place them in the plastic bowl. Enjoy this chant while you work. Invite children to rub their tummies on the last line:

Two little apples hanging in a tree.
Two little apples smiled down at me.
I shook that tree, hard as I could.
Down came the apples, mmmmm ... they were good!

BEGIN

Peel, core, and cut up the apples. Have children wash their hands, then invite them to help you make applesauce. They'll enjoy dropping the apple slices into a saucepan with an inch of water in the bottom. Cook the apples until soft. Remind children of safety rules around the stove. Occasionally remove the saucepan from the heat and carefully show children how the apples are changing color and texture. Let children smell the aroma from the pan. Encourage them to tell you what they see and smell.

Remove the cooked applesauce from the stove and let it cool. Then ask twos to help you stir the applesauce with wooden spoons. Talk about the changes that occur as children stir, modeling descriptive language: "Look, those chunky slices are all mushy now. See how smooth the applesauce is getting? The apples were white when we put them in the pan, but now they're brown." As a finishing touch, invite children to sprinkle in a little cinnamon and lemon. Watch their reactions to these wonderful smells. Help twos find words to describe them, like *spicy* and *sour*.

Time to Taste!

Now for the best part. Ask children to help spoon the applesauce into cups to enjoy together. Model more descriptive language as you talk about the delicious applesauce. Read a book about apples or about senses, such as one below, while children enjoy their snack.

Remember

■ It's hard for twos to wait until the applesauce is ready. Let them snack on apple slices while they help.
■ Keep recipes simple. Work in small steps and keep flavors mild. Most twos prefer bland foods.

BOOKS

Invite twos to see and hear these books about the senses.

■ *The Country Noisy Book* by Margaret Wise Brown (Addison-Wesley)

■ *Nibble, Nibble* by Margaret Wise Brown (Addison-Wesley)

■ *The Touch Me Book* by Pat and Eve Witte (Golden Press)

LANGUAGE

Mixing colors with play clay lets children watch — and talk about — the changes they see!

EXPERIENCING COLOR

Aim: Children will use listening, speaking, and fine-motor skills as they experiment with mixing colors.

Group size: One or two children.

Materials: Homemade play clay prepared in bright primary colors (see recipe below).

In Advance: Prepare the homemade play clay. Here is a good recipe that makes long-lasting clay: 1 cup flour, 1 cup water, 1/2 cup salt, 2 teaspoons cream of tartar, 2 tablespoons oil. Add food coloring to water, then mix all ingredients. Cook over low heat until thickened. Let cool. Make a batch each of blue, red, and yellow.

GETTING READY

Sharing a book about colors, such as one listed below, is a great way to help children become aware of colors around them. Talk about colors found in the room or in the children's clothing. Invite children to compare and match colors. Ask, "Do you see something that is the same color as this? Tell me what you see. What else is the same color?"

BEGIN

Form the play clay into small balls about one inch in diameter. Let each child choose two different-colored balls. Then leave them to knead, pull, or pound on their clay. Observe and listen as chil-

dren talk to you or to others about what they're doing. At moments when you won't interrupt their play, encourage them to verbalize their discoveries by asking what the play clay feels and smells like.

If children don't spontaneously create one big ball, ask, "What will happen if we squish the balls together? Let's try it and see." As children knead and squish, the new ball will show globs of both colors, but slowly will mix together into a new secondary color. The longer the children play with the clay, the more solid the color will become. Let children discover this on their own, but encourage them to tell you what they see happening. You'll hear their delight and surprise as they see new colors appear. Provide children with the words that describe the new colors they create — *green*, *orange*, and *purple*.

Remember

▪ It's not important for children to remember which colors made the new color or even how it happened. The essence of this activity is in observation and experimentation with change and the natural language it inspires.

▪ Develop twos' vocabulary by using color words when describing objects. In time, children will connect the word *red*, for example, with the color.

▪ A book is also a good way to follow up this activity. Share another one about colors after cleaning up. Can children find the new color they made in the book?

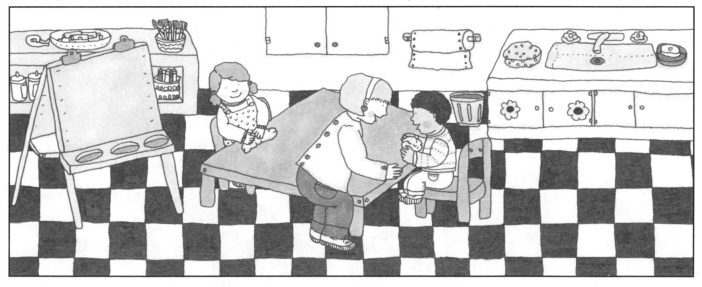

BOOKS

Here are some basic books about color.

▪ *Adventures of Three Colors* by Annette Tison and Talus Taylor (Merrill)

▪ *Colors* by Peter Schaub (Bowmar/Noble Publishing)

▪ *Little Blue and Little Yellow* by Leo Lionni (Astor Books)

LANGUAGE

Explore language and the dark with a friendly flashlight.

EXPLORING THE DARK!

Aim: Children will use listening, speaking, observation, and gross-motor skills as they explore differences between light and dark.

Group size: Three to five children.

Materials: One plastic flashlight for each child and one for you.

GETTING READY

Experiencing light and dark is a condition with which every young child is familiar. It's one that can develop language skills as children talk about what they see — or don't see.

Show children the flashlights. Let them experiment with turning the light off and on. Ask, "Have you seen a flashlight before? Who uses a flashlight at your house?" Listen as twos share their experiences with this common item. Then ask, "Can we use the flashlight to help us see in the dark?" Wait for responses, then invite twos to experiment with you.

BEGIN

Select an area you can explore as a group. It should have enough natural light so that a switch turns off the lights without making it completely dark. With the lights on, discuss objects children see — chairs, a picture, etc. Turn on the flashlights and have fun pointing the light beams at different things.

With the flashlights on, tell children that you're going to turn the lights off. Give children a few minutes to get accustomed to the change. If you sense that a child is afraid, keep him or her close to

you, reminding the child that you are near and that he is safe. Then ask, "What can you find with your flashlight? Can you find a chair? Can you find your feet?" See if anyone can find something you hadn't previously discussed. For example: "Can we shine our lights on Lisa's shoes?" or "Let's shine our flashlights on my knees!" Encourage children to talk about what they see. Point your flashlight in an area and ask, "What do you see here?"

Some children will enjoy this experience so much, they'll want to continue exploring under a table or behind the bookshelf after you turn on the room lights. Stay nearby and ask them to tell you what they find. Store the flashlights where they can be used again, with your supervision.

Share a Book

As a great follow-up to this activity, read a story together about light and dark, such as one below.

Remember

▪ Activities that interest and excite children are great language developers because children want to share their feelings and discoveries. Your sense of drama adds excitement to the exploration.

▪ As you focus on light and dark, help build children's knowledge and vocabulary by talking about objects or activities associated with light and day and with dark and night, such as the "moon that shines at night when it's dark."

▪ Avoid closets. They scare children who feel afraid when it's completely dark.

BOOKS

Share these books about light and dark, day and night.

▪ *A New Day* by Ronald Heuninck (Floris Books)

▪ *Goodnight, Goodnight* by Eve Rice (Greenwillow Books)

▪ *Light* by Donald Crews (Greenwillow Books)

<table>
<tr><td>

a b c | **LANGUAGE**

</td></tr>
</table>

LANGUAGE

Birds won't be the only ones chattering when your twos go outside to find feathered friends.

LISTEN TO THE BIRDS

Aim: Children will use listening, speaking, and gross-motor skills to describe and demonstrate what they observe as they watch bird behaviors.

Group size: Whole group, with enough adult aides so that each is responsible for three or four children.

Materials: Play binoculars or ones made from toilet-tissue rolls for each child; a book about birds; chart paper and marker; and bird feeder and seed (optional).

GETTING READY

Capitalize on an event that focuses your twos' interest on birds. For example, a child may get a bird as a pet at home. During fall or spring migrations, a flock may pass over your school or rest near

it. Or if you're really lucky, a bird may build a nest in a tree near your windows. Use this familiar creature to engage your twos in activities that involve reading, writing, listening, and speaking.

BEGIN

Go for a walk outside to an area where you know you'll see birds. Remind twos to be very quiet so they don't frighten the birds. Practice whispering. Have children use their binoculars to look for birds.

Ask, "How do you think birds move?" Ask children to compare birds' movements to their own. Narrate their actions: "Jenny runs, but birds fly," or "Mark walks, but birds fly." Children may also see birds moving in a hopping motion on the ground and picking at grass or dirt for bugs or seeds. On city streets, they may see pigeons moving with a characteristic bob of the head. Invite twos to imitate birds flying, hopping, eating, etc.

Encourage children to close their eyes and listen for bird sounds. Can they repeat the noises they hear? Listen for comments that you can expand on, either by restating what children say or by asking questions that encourage additional sharing of ideas and discoveries.

Share a Book

Follow up with a book such as *A Year of Birds* by Ashley Wolff (Dodd, Mead). Be sure each child can see clearly, and encourage twos to tell you what's in the pictures. Point out and name different parts of a bird, such as eyes, beak, wings, and feathers. Look for pictures that show what birds eat and ask twos to name what they see. Give children lots of time to share any experiences the pictures bring to mind.

Remember

■ Another way to follow up this activity is by making a brief list of what you saw immediately after your return. Invite interested children to name people, trees, birds, etc. Write each child's comments, with his or her name, on chart paper. Hang the dictations where family members will see and enjoy them.

■ To help make bird-watching an ongoing activity, hang a feeder in a tree near a window. Invite twos to help you fill the feeder with seed or to make treats for the birds, such as pinecones stuffed with peanut butter.

BOOKS

Here are more good books that feature birds.	■ *Animal Builders* by Kenneth Lilly (Random House)	■ *My Pets* by Eric Hill (Random House)	■ *Spring* by Colin McNaughton (Dial Books)

LANGUAGE A toy telephone is a rich source of language development.

TALKING ON THE TELEPHONE

Aim: Children will use listening, speaking, writing, and reading skills as they have pretend conversations on the telephone.

Group size: Two or three children.

Materials: At least two play telephones, old phone books, paper, markers, large play coins, an empty refrigerator carton, tempera paint, and paintbrushes.

In Advance: Use the refrigerator carton to make a phone booth. Stand the box upright and cut an opening on one side for a window. On another side, cut a larger opening to use as a door. Then lay the carton on one side and invite interested children to decorate the phone booth with markers or paints.

GETTING READY

Bring two toy telephones to circle time and pretend to have a conversation with someone. Invite children to take turns using the phones to have their own conversations. When everyone has had a chance to talk on the toy telephones, ask, "Do you ever talk on the telephone at home? Who do you talk to?"

Introduce the telephone booth. Ask, "Has anyone ever seen a telephone booth? Where have you seen one? Have you ever been inside one when Mommy or Daddy was making a call?" Explain that people use a pay phone in a booth to make calls when they are away from their homes. Tell children the phone booth will be set up near the dramatic-play area and that they can play with it when-ever they want.

BEGIN

Place the phone booth near your dramatic-play area, and put a chair and one telephone inside it. Place the other phone on a table in the dramatic-play area, within easy hearing of the phone booth.

Encourage pretend play by going inside the booth and calling another child. As children walk by the booth, you might tell them there is a call for them. With this type of encouragement, you'll see children use the phone booth and carry on all kinds of imagina-tive conversations.

Take a Message, Please

Add realistic props to encourage "reading" and "writing." For example, place a phone book in the booth for children to use to look up numbers. Add paper and markers by the phone in the dra-matic-play area, so that children can take messages from people who call. (As needed, model taking a message from a pretend caller to get children started.) And add large play coins for callers

to use. They'll generate interesting sound effects as children make the "ding ding" sound of coins dropping into a pay phone.

Remember

▪ Let children play in their own ways. They may not use a phone in a correct way and that's okay. The aim is to encourage lan-guage. But do discourage shouting into the phone or slamming it down in anger. Children are never too young to learn good tele-phone manners.

BOOKS

| Enjoy these books together at storytime. | ▪ *At Home* by Eric Hill (Random House) | ▪ *Harriet at Home* by Betsy and Guilio Maestro (Crown) | ▪ *Listen to That* by Zokeisha (Simon & Schuster) |

LANGUAGE

Language will flow as you explore the sensory world of touch.

FOLLOW THE "TEXTURE ROAD"

Aim: Children will use listening, speaking, and fine- and gross-motor skills in a sensory exploration.

Group size: Small groups or the whole group.

Materials: A collection of mats made from various materials such as foam rubber, rug scraps, plastic bubble wrap, doormats, linoleum, and ceramic tile; sand, plastic-foam squiggles, or smooth pebbles glued onto sheets of cardboard; and quiet instrumental recordings.

In Advance: Invite a few children to help you prepare a "texture road" by placing the mats in an interesting, winding pattern. Try to alternate textures so children can make comparisons easily.

GETTING READY

Encourage children to touch their clothes, hair, and skin, and describe how each feels. Introduce words such as *hard*, *soft*, *rough*, and *smooth* to help them, but encourage their imaginative made-up words, too.

BEGIN

Invite children to sit on the floor along the texture road. Introduce the road and talk about what materials make up the different mats. Encourage children to feel and describe the surfaces and to name items they recognize, such as sand or stones.

Now invite children to take off their shoes and socks and take turns walking down the texture road, beginning at one end. Put on soft background music. As the children step on each different texture, ask them to describe what it feels like.

As a variation, let children walk in pairs. Suggest that one child close his or her eyes while the other leads her, then for the pair to change roles and walk along the road again. Talk about whether walking with eyes closed changes how each texture feels.

Play the Toes-to-Toes Game

Try this cooperative game: It's a great way for children to learn body parts. Divide children into pairs. Explain that when you name a body part, children touch that part of their bodies to the same part on their partners. For example, if you call out, "toes to toes," pairs touch toes. Start with simple parts such as heads, hands, arms, knees, noses, etc.

Remember

■ Leave the texture road out for a few days so threes can try it again on their own. This novel experience will generate a lot of interesting language.

BOOKS

Here are some great books to continue your talks about touch and textures.

■ *Find Out by Touching* by Paul Showers (Thomas Y. Crowell)

■ *Fingers Are Always Bringing Me News* by Mary O'Neill (Doubleday)

■ *My Bunny Feels Soft* by Charlotte Steiner (Alfred A. Knopf)

LANGUAGE

Your threes will want to play these games again and again.

LET'S PLAY CIRCLE GAMES!

Aim: Children will use listening, speaking, and gross-motor skills while playing simple games together.
Group size: Small groups or the whole group.
Materials: None.

GETTING READY

Play a familiar circle game together, such as "Ring Around the Rosie." Show children how to walk in a circle holding hands, then say the rhyme and encourage children to join in:

Ring around the rosie.
A pocket full of posies.
Ashes, ashes, we all fall down!
(Everyone falls to the ground.)

As you know, threes love circling, falling down, and getting up again. Give them time to play this game over and over.

BEGIN

Now that children are familiar with a circle game, introduce a new one, such as this British favorite, "Sally Go 'Round the Sun." Children walk around the circle holding hands. When they say "BOOM!" they fall down, then quickly pop up and go around the circle again in the opposite direction.

Sally Go 'Round the Sun
(Chant the words or sing to "Looby Loo" tune.)
Sally go 'round the sun.
Sally go 'round the moon.
Sally go 'round the chimney top.
Every afternoon, BOOM!!

Try Another One!

The old favorite "Looby Loo" is also popular with threes. It's similar to "Hokey Pokey" because it asks children to put parts of their bodies in the circle.

Looby Loo
(Children circle around as they sing.)
Here we go looby loo.
Here we go looby lie.
Here we go looby loo.
All on a Saturday night.

I put my hand in.
I take my hand out.
I give myself a shake, shake, shake,
And turn myself about.

Repeat the first verse each time before substituting a new body part in the second verse. Encourage children to suggest different body parts.

Remember

• These are wonderful games to play often. As children become more familiar with the words and actions, they'll enjoy them more and more.
• Young children are delighted by nonsense words like *looby loo*. Chants and circle games are a great way to introduce them to the rhyme and rhythm of language.

BOOKS

Check these books for other circle games.

• *Holiday Singing and Dancing Games* by Esther Nelson (Sterling)

• *The Puffin Song Book* by Leslie Woodgate (Puffin Books)

• *Singing and Dancing Games for the Very Young* by Esther Nelson (Sterling)

a b c | **LANGUAGE**

Threes will have a lot of rhyming fun with their favorite animals.

ANIMAL RHYMES

Aim: Children will use listening, speaking, and motor skills as they act out rhymes about familiar animals.

Group size: Whole group.

Materials: Pictures or plastic or stuffed toys of familiar animals, chart paper, a marker, lively instrumental music, and a record or tape player.

GETTING READY

Gather children in a circle. Show pictures or stuffed or plastic toys of favorite animals. Talk about the animals. Which are children's favorites? Does someone have another kind of animal that they like better? List all responses on chart paper. Invite children to

demonstrate how the different animals they've named move and sound.

Play some lively music and invite the whole group to move like different animals on the chart. Ask, "Can you slither like a snake? Can you hop like a kangaroo? Can you run on your hands and knees like a dog?" Give children plenty of time to act out these various motions in their own ways. Listen for their use of your descriptive words, like *slither*.

BEGIN

Now introduce these delightful animal rhymes. Encourage children to use whatever hand and body motions they want to act out each rhyme. If possible, substitute some of your children's favorite animals for those mentioned.

Like the Animals
Hop like a bunny.
Crawl like cat.
Squeak like a mouse.
I can do that!

My Bear
I love my bear,
And he loves me.
While he eats honey,
I drink tea.
Come visit us,
And we'll be three!

Puppies
Puppies jump
And roll around.
And then they sleep all day.
They lick your nose,
And tickle your toes,
And play and play and play!

Remember
▪ Do these often. The more familiar children become with the words, the more fun they'll have with the rhymes.
▪ Enjoy other favorite animal fingerplays and rhymes together: "Two Little Blackbirds," "Baa Baa Black Sheep," "Five Little Monkeys," "Pop Goes the Weasel," etc.

BOOKS

Share these delightful books about animals together.

▪ *Baby Farm Animals* by Garth Williams (Western)

▪ *Good Morning Chick,* retold by Mirra Ginsburg (Greenwillow Books)

▪ *Our Animal Friends at Maple Hill Farm* by Alice and Martin Provensen (Random House)

LANGUAGE

Drip, drop, swish, splash — everyday sounds help children develop listening skills.

TAKE A LISTENING WALK

Aim: Children will use listening, speaking, and gross-motor skills in an auditory exploration.

Group size: Four to six children or the whole group.

Materials: Chart paper and marker, and a portable tape recorder.

In Advance: Over the course of a few days, help children get in tune with sounds by pointing out and describing sounds as they occur. For example: "Wow, Louis, your car makes a loud, roaring sound when you move it." Or, "Cynthia, can you hear the wind blowing? It makes a whooshing sound."

GETTING READY

Invite children to take a "listening walk." Unless the weather is inclement, go outdoors. Otherwise, stroll around indoors. To help focus children's attention on sounds before your walk, ask a few open-ended questions such as, "What kinds of sounds do you think we will hear on our walk? Where should we go to hear lots of sounds?" Write down children's predictions on chart paper, and check them again when you return from the walk.

Take along a portable tape recorder to record sounds you hear. Later, you can play back the tape and invite children to try to identify the sounds.

BEGIN

A listening walk should be a leisurely stroll. Stop now and then so children can focus on the sounds around them. Encourage them to tell you about the sounds they hear, and help them use descriptive words such as *banging*, *roaring*, *ringing*, etc. Look for the source of each sound. When one isn't in sight, ask children to guess what might be making the mystery sound. Have fun and make the walk an adventure!

Imitate Sounds

After the walk, sit together and talk about the sounds you heard. Invite children to try to re-create the sounds using only their voices, and acknowledge their efforts: "Yes, Lindsay, that sounds like the bird we heard." Or, "Shakeela, that does sound like water running in the sink."

Sing a Sound Song!

Sing this song (to the tune of "Did You Ever See a Lassie?") after your walk. Substitute objects and sounds the children identified for those in the song.

> *Did you ever hear a bell ring,*
> *A bell ring, a bell ring?*
> *Did you ever hear a bell ring?*
> *Ding, dong, ding, ding, dong.*
>
> *Did you ever hear the wind blow,*
> *The wind blow, the wind blow?*
> *Did you ever hear the wind blow?*
> *Swish, swish, swish, swish, swish.*

Remember

▪ Listening to sounds and re-creating them are separate skills. Children need lots of practice with the first before they try the second.

BOOKS

Threes will love these books about sounds and words.

▪ *Richard Scarry's Just Right Word Book* by Richard Scarry (Random House)

▪ *Sounds* by David Bennett (Bantam Little Rooster)

▪ *Spot's Big Book of Words* by Eric Hill (Putnam Publishing Group)

a b c LANGUAGE

Threes are fascinated with tiny things, so use tiny objects to inspire conversation.

TALKING "TINY" TALK

Aim: Children will use listening, speaking, creative thinking, comparison, and seriation skills in an imaginative activity.

Group size: Four children.

Materials: A collection of very small objects, such as miniature toys, dolls, furniture, and dishes; an old glove; felt for features; and chart paper and markers.

In Advance: Send a letter to parents asking them to help their child look at home for a small object he or she would like to share with the group. Explain that as part of a language activity on a particular day, children will be talking about tiny things. Ask parents to send each item in a small bag or box, so that it won't get lost. Test each object with a choke tube. Keep those that don't pass the test on a high shelf, and bring them down for show only, not for play.

Cut off the pinky finger of an old glove to make a tiny finger puppet. Sew on simple felt features.

GETTING READY

Introduce the concept of "tiny" by showing children a few miniature objects. Share a book about a tiny person or object, such as *The Teeny-Tiny Woman* by Paul Galdone (Clarion Books). Then bring out Tiny, your pinky puppet, a special little friend. Invite children to sing this song with Tiny, using a "little" voice.

Tiny's Song
(Tune: "Where Is Thumbkin?" Use traditional hand motions.)
Where is Tiny?
Where is Tiny?
Here I am.
Here I am.
You are very tiny.
You are very tiny.
Yes, I am.
Yes, I am.

BEGIN

Now invite children to take turns sharing their tiny objects from home. Ask a child to unwrap her item and tell about it, using open-ended questions to encourage the child to be descriptive. For example: "Does your object have a name? What do you do with it?"

Encourage children to compare their tiny objects. Help them notice that not all tiny objects are the same size. Ask children to pick the smallest object and the largest. Suggest that they carefully arrange the objects in a row from the smallest to the largest.

When everyone has shared their tiny objects, plan a snack of tiny crackers and pour juice into bathroom-sized paper cups. While children enjoy their snacks, invite them to tell about the tiniest thing they've ever seen — a bug, flower, etc. List children's responses on chart paper, then reread the list, marveling at all the tiny things they've seen!

Remember

▪ Don't expect threes to have a firm understanding of what *tiny* really means. Through experiences like this, their understanding of size will be refined.

BOOKS

| Take tiny talk a step further with these books. | ▪ *The Funny Little Woman* by Arlen Mosel (E.P. Dutton) | ▪ *The Prince of Dolomites* by Tomie dePaola (Harcourt Brace Jovanovich) | ▪ *A Tiny Family* by Norman Bridwell (Scholastic) |

LANGUAGE

Get your threes talking with interesting props to see, touch, and match.

THE GO-TOGETHER GAME

Aim: Children will use listening, speaking, problem-solving, and creative-thinking skills as they match objects.

Group size: Three or four children.

Materials: Several pairs of familiar objects that go together, such as a baseball and a plastic bat, a fork and spoon, a toy car and toy truck, a doll and doll clothes, and paper and a crayon; and a pillowcase or paper bag.

GETTING READY

Introduce the idea of "going together" by inviting children to clap their hands. Say, "Our hands go together when we clap. Let's try it. Now try to clap with one hand. See?" Encourage children to look for objects around them that go together, such as feet and shoes, heads and hats, and tables and chairs.

BEGIN

Put your collection of items into a pillowcase or paper bag. Bring children together in a circle and pass the bag to the first child. Invite him or her to pull out an item, name it, and place it where everyone can see it. Talk about how the item is used. Then pass the bag to the next child so that she can do the same. Give children time to tell what they know about each item, and continue to pass the bag until it is empty.

Next, look over the collection of items together. Hold up one object and ask, "Who can find something that goes with this?" When a match is made, help a child use descriptive language to explain why the items go together. (Some children may prefer to show why by demonstrating how the items are used.) Remember, there may be different ways items can be paired with each other. Listen to children's explanations. They may think of reasons you won't.

Sing the Go-Together Song

Sing this song each time a new match is made. The tune is "Mulberry Bush."

> *Bats and balls, they go together,*
> *Go together,*
> *Go together.*
> *Bats and balls, they go together,*
> *Just like bread and butter!*

Match Again Another Day

This can be an intriguing ongoing activity for children. Place a bag of pairs of items that go together in your manipulative area. Let children examine the items and make their matches on their own. You might join a child occasionally and ask her to tell you why she paired up items as she did. Encourage flexible thinking by inviting the child to look for new ways to match the same items into different pairs.

Remember

▪ You are exploring together, not looking for "right" answers. Listen to children's ideas and accept them, even if their logic is different than yours. You can inhibit language if children sense you're looking for a particular answer.

BOOKS

As you share these books, be on the lookout for more "go-togethers."	▪ *The Cupboard* by John Burningham (Thomas Y. Crowell)	▪ *Harriet at Play* by Betsy and Giulio Maestro (Crown)	▪ *The Supermarket* by Anne and Harlow Rockwell (Macmillan)

<table>

| a b c LANGUAGE | **Get to know your children and their families better.** |

</table>

ALL MY FRIENDS AND FAMILY

Aim: Children will use listening and speaking skills as they talk about the people in their lives.

Group size: One child.

Materials: Pictures of families and family members from magazines; construction paper; a stapler; and paste or tape.

In Advance: Send a note home, asking parents to send in a few pictures of family members who are important to their child. Be sure parents label the back of the pictures to ensure safe return.

GETTING READY

Sit with a child in a comfortable, cozy place. Talk about your family and the people and possibly animals who are important to you. Use short sentences, beginning with just two or three names: "I live with Don. My dog Brandy is my special friend. My best friend, Maryann, lives in another house." You may even have pictures you'll want to share.

BEGIN

Invite the child to tell you about people and animals who are special to him or her. If the child has brought pictures from home, look at them together. Ask the child to tell who is in the pictures and what he thinks the people may be doing. Help him use relationship words such as *uncle*, *stepfather*, *grandmother*, and *sister*. Encourage the child to share remembrances of each person that the photos bring to mind. This can be a wonderful sharing time and

one that builds a bond of closeness between you and the child as he brings you into his home world.

Make a Families Display

Place magazines showing families (in various configurations) from different ethnic groups in or near your art area. Let children go through the magazines on their own to look for pictures that remind them of their own family members. Work with individual children, cutting out pictures the child chooses or letting the child tear out the pictures on his own. Then help him paste or tape them to a large piece of construction paper.

Talk about the pictures the child has selected and invite him to name and tell about the people in the pictures. Write the names, exactly as the child says them, next to the appropriate person or pet. Hang at eye level. Over time, children may also want to add more pictures of people they identify as neighbors, friends, and other relatives. This can become an "Important People Corner" in your room.

Remember

▪ Children need and like to talk about those who care for and are close to them. Concrete reminders, like photos or magazine pictures that children can look at and touch, provide comfort — helping children to feel more secure when they're away from their families.

BOOKS

| Share these books about different types of families. | ▪ *The Birthday Thing* by SuAnn and Kevin Kiser (Greenwillow Books) | ▪ *Hello Baby* by Charlotte Doyle (Random House) | ▪ *I Go With My Family to Grandma's* by Rikki Levinson (E.P. Dutton) |

a b c LANGUAGE

What's that sound? Let's listen and find out.

WHAT'S THAT SOUND?

Aim: Children will use listening, speaking, motor, and observation skills in an auditory exploration.

Group size: Three or four children.

Materials: Objects that make sounds that are fairly easy for children to recognize, such as rattles, keys, and a tambourine; and a folding screen, curtain, or large box to hide behind.

In Advance: Send a letter home telling parents that for the next few days you will be focusing on listening skills. Ask them to encourage their child to be aware of sounds and to try to identify sounds together. Then ask parents to help each child find an object to bring to school that makes a sound that other threes can guess easily. Remind families to bring the objects in a bag or box so that each remains a secret.

GETTING READY

Share a book about sounds, such as one listed below. When you finish, ask children to listen for sounds in the room. What do they hear? Are there sounds coming from their own bodies? Is anyone's stomach growling? Try swallowing together. What do children hear? Then get ready for children to share their mystery sound objects. If there are children who don't have an object from home, help them find a noisemaker in the room they can use.

BEGIN

You can play this game in small groups or get the whole group together. (According to children's attention spans, you may want to play the sound game several times during the day.) Set up a screen, curtain, or box to hide behind.

Demonstrate what to do by going behind the screen with a few objects that make sounds children will recognize easily. Make the sounds one at a time. Ask children to guess what object is making each sound. If children guess correctly, ask, "How did you know what made that sound when you couldn't see what I was holding?" If they have trouble guessing a sound, give them clues about the object you're using.

Now invite children to take turns standing behind the screen and using their mystery object to make a sound. Stand next to the screen so you can assist the child as needed. If children have difficulty identifying a sound, ask the child making the sound to offer some clues. (Help the child come up with descriptive words as needed.) Once someone has guessed the object, ask the child to show the object so everyone can make a visual connection.

Remember

▪ Threes may have a difficult time identifying sounds made with unusual objects. Vary the game by giving children visual clues. For example, ask three children to show their objects to the group. Then ask all three children to take their objects behind the screen, but only make a noise with one of the objects. Children can try to figure out which of the three objects made the noise.

▪ Good listening skills develop with time. Emphasize the importance of listening in all activities. When giving directions, use simple, clear language.

BOOKS

Sound off with these great books!

▪ *A Crowd of Crows* by John Graham (Scholastic)

▪ *Listen! Listen!* by Ann and Paul Rand (Harcourt Brace Jovanovich)

▪ *Listen to That!* by H. Klurfmeier (Western)

LANGUAGE

Encourage your threes' verbal skills while you experiment with finger paints.

MUSHING, GUSHING, AND TALKING

Aim: Children will use listening, speaking, fine-motor, and creative skills as they do an art activity.

Group size: Three or four children.

Materials: Finger-paint paper, dishes of warm water, powdered gelatin, self-seal plastic bags, food coloring, liquid finger paint, spoons, and a tape recorder (optional).

GETTING READY

When children have their hands in something, language seems to flow! Ask them to wash their hands. (Some threes like this part best!) Give each child finger-paint paper. Talk about what it might feel like to paint with your fingers.

BEGIN

Ask each child to drip a small amount of warm water onto the paper. Encourage them to talk about the way the water feels as they spread it around. Now give each a few spoonfuls of gelatin to sprinkle on the water. Let them choose a color of food coloring and add a few drops. Listen and observe as children see and feel changes in the gelatin. Help them focus on the way the mixture looks, feels, and smells as they move and mix the gelatin and water together. (It will go from lumpy to slippery.)

When each child is finished, use a clean sheet of paper to make a print of his or her creation. If the child wants to, invite her to dictate something about the picture or about the experience of paint-

ing with gelatin. Write her words on a separate sheet of paper, to attach to the picture. Be sure to have children wash their hands after this sticky activity.

Mush and Gush Bags

Here's a fun way to mix finger-paint colors. Ask children to help you fill reusable plastic storage bags with a few spoonfuls of two different colors of finger paint. Help them seal the bags. (Secure the bags by putting a strip of tape over the seal.) Invite children to talk about the colors. Let them experiment with ways they could "paint" by moving the colors around inside the bag. Listen to their comments and explanations of what's happening as the colors mix together. Some children may want to add a third color to their bags. Encourage them to predict what might happen when they do.

Remember

• The pictures children create don't need to be of anything. The excitement of this activity is in the process, not the product.

• You may want to record children's comments on tape as they finger-paint with gelatin or as they see the colors in their mushing bags mix. Later, you can play the tape back for children. Encourage them to try to identify each other's voices. Transcribe the comments to share with family members.

• Some children may want to empty the contents of their bags onto finger-paint paper to create new pictures.

BOOKS

Enhance language skills when you talk about these great word-less picture books.

• *Bobo's Dream* by Martha Alexander (Dial Books)

• *Bubble Bubble* by Mercer Mayer (Parents Magazine Press)

• *Look What I Can Do* by Jose Aruego (Charles Scribner's Sons)

a b c LANGUAGE

Spark creative thinking and inspire your budding artists with a repeating poem.

"IN THE DARK, DARK ..."

Aim: Children will use listening, speaking, writing, and fine-motor skills and creative expression.

Group size: Four or five children.

Materials: Squares of oaktag, crayons, black tempera paint (thickened with liquid detergent), large paper clips, construction paper, chart paper, and markers.

GETTING READY

Share this version of the poem "In the Dark, Dark Woods." Children love the predictable, repetitive language and will delight in saying it over and over:

> In the dark, dark woods there's a
> Dark, dark cave.
> In the dark, dark cave there's a
> Dark, dark tree.
> In the dark, dark tree there's a
> Dark, dark hole.
> In the dark, dark hole there's a
> Dark, dark nest.
> In the dark, dark nest there's a
> Dark, dark baby monster.
> Looking at me!

Ask, "What do you think the dark, dark woods look like?" Give children plenty of time to respond with their ideas, and continue with other questions about the cave, tree, etc. Then invite interested children to create their own "dark, dark" pictures.

BEGIN

Give each child a piece of oaktag and crayons. Encourage children to press hard and to color every part of the paper. (Most will launch into this with gusto!) Then invite children to cover their pictures with black paint to make them "dark, dark." Listen to their comments as they watch what happens.

While the paint is still wet, encourage children to use large paper clips to draw lines, designs, or pictures on the paint. The crayon colors will show through, creating an interesting effect. Let dry, then mount the pictures on construction paper and display. Invite children to tell you about their pictures. Record their words to display near the artwork.

Make Up a Poem

The repetitive language of "In the Dark, Dark Woods" makes it perfect for creating new variations. Work with a small group. Suggest a first line such as "In a tiny, tiny house" or "In a quiet, quiet room," and invite children to add other lines. Write the new poem on chart paper, and share it with all your fours.

Remember

▪ Don't insist that the pictures relate to the poem. Let children create in their own ways. Some may enjoy the poem but won't want to do a picture at all.

▪ This poem can encourage some wonderful dramatic play. Help interested children create a cave (an old blanket thrown over a table or a support made of large blocks). Listen to the language this setting inspires!

BOOKS

Encourage fours to join in as you read these predictable stories.

▪ *A Ghost Story* by Bill Martin Jr. (Holt, Rinehart & Winston)

▪ *If You Give a Mouse a Cookie* by Laura Joffe Numeroff (Scholastic Big Books)

▪ *What Do You Do With a Kangaroo?* by Mercer Mayer (Scholastic Big Books)

LANGUAGE

Music + Poetry = Fun for Fours!

RHYME AND RHYTHM

Aim: Children will use listening, speaking, reading, and gross-motor skills in a rhyming activity.

Group size: Any size.

Materials: Chart paper, marker, instrumental music, and a children's rhyming book.

GETTING READY

Read aloud a simple poem or a nursery rhyme that your fours know. Recite the words with feeling, so children begin to feel the movement and rhythm of the verse. Move your hands, feet, or head to the beat of the words and invite children to do the same. Recite the poem several times, encouraging fours to join in.

BEGIN

Play some instrumental music and give children time to move freely to it. Lower the music and read the poem aloud as the music plays in the background. Encourage children to move to the music and words of the poem. Talk about how the words and music make you feel — funny, silly, happy, etc.

Rhyme Time

Some children will enjoy focusing on just the rhyming words

themselves. Slowly read the poem again, emphasizing the rhyming words. Can children think of other real or made-up words that rhyme with those in the poem? Create a list on chart paper. Later, if children are moving to the poem again, challenge them to make up a special movement of their own when they hear words that rhyme.

Make a Poetry Chart

Reread the poem as you write the words on a large piece of chart paper. Add simple drawings for the most important words to help children "read" the poem on their own. Hang the chart low, where children can see and refer to it.

Remember

▪ Fingerplays and song lyrics are also forms of poetry. Have fun incorporating many forms of lyrical verse into all areas of your curriculum.

▪ Young children often create rhymes spontaneously while playing. Record these exactly as children say them and share them again at circle time.

▪ Nonsense words and rhymes help children — and adults — to appreciate the pure joy of language!

BOOKS

Here are good books of poetry and rhyme to use with fours.

▪ *The Dog Laughed* by Lucy Cousins (E.P. Dutton)

▪ *Gorilla/Chinchilla* by Bert Kitchen (Dial Books)

▪ *Still as a Star* by Lee Bennett Hopkins (Little, Brown)

abc **LANGUAGE**

Familiar objects can inspire so much language!

LOTS AND LOTS OF SHOES

Aim: Children will use listening, speaking, reading, writing, gross-motor, and creative-thinking skills as they focus on a fun and favorite item — shoes.

Group size: Four or five children.

Materials: A variety of shoes such as ballet shoes, work boots, high heels, sneakers, silly slippers, etc.; empty shoeboxes; and note paper and markers.

In Advance: Send a note home to families inviting them to donate old shoes and empty shoeboxes to add to your dress-up collection. If possible, borrow a shoe sizer from a local shoe store.

GETTING READY

Talk about the different types of shoes children are wearing, and encourage them to identify similarities and differences. Count how many children have shoes with laces and how many have shoes without laces. Ask children to explain how the shoes without laces stay on. Encourage fours to share their experiences with going to a store to buy shoes.

BEGIN

Place any newly acquired shoes in the dress-up area. Observe as children try on the shoes and use them as costumes for different roles. Join children in the dress-up area, and at moments when you won't disrupt play, talk about the different pairs of shoes. Encourage children to tell you about who they're pretending to be as they wear them.

Create a Shoe Store

Add other props that may inspire new play scenarios, such as empty shoeboxes and a shoe sizer. Children may want to create a shoe store in the theme area, with players taking turns being customers and salespeople. (You may need to demonstrate how to use the shoe sizer to measure feet.) Let children take the lead in creating their shoe store, assisting only as needed. For example, you may be asked to create a sign that says "Shoe Store," or a child may want you to write the words for him to copy on a sign. Provide paper and markers that children can use to make price tags, write up orders, or give as receipts. The potential for all areas of language development — speaking, listening, writing, and reading — in a creative scenario like this is endless!

Play the "Imaginary Shoes" Game

Here's a delightful movement activity that builds on children's

interest in shoes. Play some light instrumental music to encourage movement. Ask children to imagine that they are wearing big heavy boots, and encourage them to tell you how they would walk in those boots. Try out those movements, then change the imaginary boots to flippers, high heels, a giant's shoes, ice skates, etc. Help children attach descriptive words to their movements, such as *clomping, stomping, flitting, twirling, sliding,* and *gliding.* End the play on a quiet note by pretending to put on warm, fluffy slippers and inviting children to curl up for a "bedtime story" about shoes, such as one below.

Remember

▪ Be sure that all shoes are clean. It may be necessary to use a spray disinfectant.

▪ Be sure to let children create and play out scenarios in their own ways. When they feel inspired and excited by a theme, you'll see more meaningful play and hear the language flow.

BOOKS

| More shoes? Why not! Fours will enjoy these stories. | ▪ *New Blue Shoes* by Eve Rice (Viking Penguin) | ▪ *Shoes* by Elizabeth Winthrop (Harper & Row) | ▪ *What Can You Do With a Shoe?* by Beatrice de Regniers (Harper & Row) |

Fours and puppets go hand in hand.

SOCK IT TO ME!

Aim: Children will use listening, speaking, and fine-motor skills and creative expression as they make puppets, then use them to tell stories.

Group size: Four or five children.

Materials: Old, clean socks; felt or construction-paper scraps; non-toxic white glue; crayons or markers; scissors; chart paper; and a tape recorder.

GETTING READY

Invite each child in your small group to choose a book from the library corner. Look through the books together and decide on one favorite. Read the book aloud. Then invite children to use the pictures as visual clues to help them retell the story in their own words. Record their words as they say them, both on tape and in print on chart paper. Display the chart-paper story to share with the whole group and with family members. Play back the tape for the storytellers, and let them listen again on their own as often as they like.

BEGIN

Show children the old socks and other puppet-making materials and invite them to make simple puppets to use to act out the story. Talk about the characters they'll need and let each child choose a character to make. If there are more characters than children, you might play several small roles or invite other children to join in. If there are more puppeteers than roles, encourage children to make up some new characters to add to the story.

Give children plenty of time to create their characters using paper and felt scraps, scissors, markers, and glue. Observe as they try on the sock puppets and experiment with ways to make them "talk."

Performance Time

When the puppets are ready, invite children to use them to tell the story. They may choose to play the tape and act out the lines they hear, or to retell the story from memory, using new dialogue. Let them develop the puppet show in their own way.

While a stage isn't necessary, some children will enjoy the excitement of performing in a theater setting. Here are ideas for three simple "stages":
▪ Table theater: Turn a table on its side; children sit behind it so puppets are seen by the audience.
▪ Doorway theater: Tack a sheet or towel across the lower part of a

doorway — not a fire exit — so children can sit or kneel behind it.
▪ Window theater: On a warm day, puppeteers can stand outside a low, open window while peers watch inside.

Remember

▪ When retelling a story, children may stray from the original plot or story line. Go with it. Memorizing the story isn't what matters. And the freer children feel, the more imaginative their language and ideas will be. They may come up with some great plot twists!
▪ Puppets are wonderful language developers. Encourage children who enjoy these activities to create other kinds of puppets and stories to act out.

BOOKS			
Children often enjoy retelling these favorites.	▪ *Caps for Sale* by Esphyr Slobodkina (Addison-Wesley)	▪ *The Gingerbread Boy* illustrated by Stephanie Birch (Ideals)	▪ *Stone Soup* by Marcia Brown (Macmillan)

 LANGUAGE   **Fours will be delighted with this language lesson.**

HOLA MEANS *HELLO*

Aim: Children will use listening and speaking skills, and enhance awareness of other places and peoples.

Group size: Small groups or whole group.

Materials: Pictures of people and everyday situations in the countries on which you will be focusing.

In Advance: Learn to say "hello" in languages that will be meaningful and interesting to your children. Here are some examples: Spanish, *hola* (ola); French, *bonjour* (bonjer); German, *guten tag* (gooten tog); Hebrew, *shalom* (shalome); Italian, *saluto* (salooto); Japanese, *koneecheesa*; Chinese, *neehow.*

GETTING READY

Invite an adult (if possible someone from one of your children's families) who speaks another language to visit. Ask the guest to teach the children how to say hello in that language, as well as other simple words. (Decide with the person ahead of time what those words will be. Stay nearby to assist the guest as needed.)

Talk with children to gauge their understanding and interest in why people speak different languages. Invite children who know words in other languages to share them. Ask children if they can think of ways they could communicate with someone who speaks another language without using words. Invite them to pantomime actions for "Hello," "Go that way," "Sit down here," "I like you," and phrases children think of.

BEGIN

Every few days during circle time, greet children with the word for hello in a different language. Sing this "Hello Song" together to introduce the new word:

> *Hello, hello,*
> *Hello and how are you?*
> *I'm fine.*
> *I'm fine.*
> *And I hope that you are, too.*
>
> *Hola, hola.*
> *Hola and how are you?*
> *I'm fine.*
> *I'm fine.*
> *And I hope that you are, too.*

Share pictures and books about a country where the language is spoken, and invite children to share anything they know about that place. Say "hello" in your new way throughout the day.

Remember

- Include the languages spoken by all of the children in your group, but be sensitive to those who are not comfortable "teaching" peers their native language.
- Don't expect children to pronounce words in other languages perfectly. But do model for children respect for the languages and customs of others.
- Make sure that any pictures you share with children are free of stereotypes.

BOOKS

| These books will also help children learn about other peoples and places. | ■ *Akimba and the Magic Crow!* by Anne Rose (Scholastic) | ■ *The Animal Peace Day* by Jan Wahl (Crown) | ■ *The Bridge* by Ralph Steadman (Doubleday) |

a b c **LANGUAGE**

Then what do we do? A review of daily activities gets everyone talking.

OUR DAY AT SCHOOL

Aim: Children will use listening, speaking, reading, creative-thinking, and sequencing skills as they create a book about their day at school.
Group size: Four or five children.
Materials: Chart paper and an instant camera; construction paper, crayons, and markers; and an empty photo album.

GETTING READY

Ask children to name all the different activities they do at school as you list them on chart paper. Add a simple drawing as a visual clue beside each word. Review the list together, and invite children to tell about their favorite parts of the day.

BEGIN

Invite each small group of children to create pages that will go in a whole-group picture book about a day at school. Show children the instant camera and assure them that every child who wants to may, with your assistance, take a picture of an activity. Invite "artists" to also draw pictures to go in the book.

Take photos of children during a day's events. (Make sure that everyone gets in at least a few pictures.) Invite your photographers to hold the camera and help you decide what shots to take. Aim for a sampling of many activities.

Children will be anxious to see the pictures, so sit back and enjoy them together. You'll hear wonderful conversations as the children see themselves and their friends in photos.

Make a Class Book

Mount each photo and picture on a separate sheet of construction paper. Let the children decide what to say about each picture. Write their comments on separate sheets of construction paper or under each photo. (Let the individual artists dictate descriptions to go with their drawings.)

Spread out the pictures so children can see them clearly, then ask children to help you arrange the pictures to show the order of events in their day. Start with a picture that shows the first thing that happens at school, and place it on the first page of a photo album obtained for this purpose. Then ask, "What do we do next?" and place this picture on the second page. Continue until all the pictures have been sequenced (more or less) correctly. Finish by adding a title on the album cover, such as "Our Day at School."

Share the book with children at storytime. Place it in your library corner so that children can look at it again and again. Share

it with their families, too, at school or at home.

Remember

- The more involved children feel in the process of creating this book, the more meaningful it will be. Resist the temptation to make it perfect. A fuzzy photo or a picture or two out of order will not diminish the memories and language this book will encourage.
- Place the book where visitors can see it, too. It's a delightful way to tell others about your program.

BOOKS

Share other books about school with your fours.

- *Calico Cat at School* by Donald Charles (Children's Press)

- *Shawn Goes to School* by Petronella Breinburg (Thomas Y. Crowell)

- *Welcome Roberto* by Mary Serfozo (Follett)

 LANGUAGE **Old greeting cards can be a gold mine of language!**

TURN CARDS INTO BOOKS

Aim: Children will use listening, speaking, reading, writing, and fine-motor skills and creative expression as they make their own books.

Group size: Three or four children.

Materials: Decorative covers from old greeting cards; white drawing paper and construction paper; non-toxic white glue; crayons or markers; and a stapler.

GETTING READY

Share a wordless picture book with children, and invite them to help you tell the story by describing what they see happening in the pictures. Emphasize that all stories have a beginning and an end by asking children to recall what happened in the first picture and in the last. Use situations where children may see different things in the same picture to point out that a story told from pictures can be told in many different ways. Then invite interested children to create their own picture books to "read" to others.

BEGIN

Show children the greeting cards, choose a few, and invite them to help you tell a story based on those pictures. Then ask each child to choose three or four cards to use as illustrations for their own books. Encourage them to experiment with the sequence of the pictures to make a story they like.

Next, give children white paper on which to glue the pictures to create book pages. If children want to add words to their books, help them position each card so there's some room at the bottom of the paper for a line or two of text. Provide crayons for children to add their own drawings, decorations, or words on the pages. Invite children who want to dictate a story to tell it to you or to another adult. (Always transcribe children's exact words.)

Create a Cover

Show children the covers from several books, and talk about what's on each. Mention the illustration, title, and author's name.

Invite children to create covers for their books. Some may want to make up a title to dictate to you. Others may just want to write their name on the cover. Let children add illustrations in whatever way they like. As a final step, staple the cover and inside pages of each book together.

Sharing Books

Encourage your authors to take turns sharing their books with

the group. Pass the books around so children can see them up close.

Remember

▪ Creativity counts most, not product. Help children feel proud of their efforts, so that they'll want to share their books with family and friends. That's how their language skills will grow.

▪ Greeting-card books make great gifts for children to give family members on special days or anytime.

▪ Some children will be too shy to share their book with a group, so invite them to "read" to you.

BOOKS

These are wonderful wordless books to share with children.	▪ *Changes, Changes* by Pat Hutchins (Macmillan)	▪ *Do You Want to Be My Friend?* by Eric Carle (Thomas Y. Crowell)	▪ *Pancakes for Breakfast* by Tomie dePaola (Harcourt Brace Jovanovich)

a b c LANGUAGE

Fours will enjoy thinking and talking as they consider a fascinating question.

WHAT IF ANIMALS COULD TALK?

Aim: Children will use listening, speaking, reading, writing, observing, and creative-thinking skills as they have fun imagining.

Group size: Three or four children.

Materials: Magazine pictures of animals, drawing paper, markers and crayons, paste, animal stickers, rubber animal stamps and stamp pads, and paper bags; old, clean socks; and scrap craft materials.

GETTING READY

As children's own communication skills are developing, focusing on how animals communicate can be a meaningful activity. Begin by giving children time to observe animal behaviors. You might take children on a walk to watch animals such as birds and squirrels, or visit a pet shop or zoo and watch how animals interact with humans or with other animals. You might also study your own pet or borrow a pet to observe for a few days. Draw on children's own experiences, too.

Talk with children as they observe. Ask, "Can you tell when an animal is happy? How do you know when an animal is scared?" Help fours notice how animals use sounds and movements to tell others what they feel or need.

BEGIN

Now encourage children to use those firsthand observations in imaginative ways. Ask, "What if animals could talk? What do you think they would say?" Invite children to think about the animals they have observed and, together, brainstorm things these animals might say if they could talk.

Creating Picture Captions

Show children the collection of magazine pictures you have gathered. Look especially for pictures from pet-food ads, which often show animals with funny expressions or in unlikely situations. Let each child choose one. Provide paper, glue, animal stickers, stamps and stamp pads, crayons, and markers for children to use to glue the pictures to heavy paper. They can add drawings or dictate words that tell what each animal is saying or thinking. (You might write their words in dialogue balloons, like those used in comic strips.) Leave out the magazines so children can look for other pictures they want to caption.

Invite children to share their pictures and captions with others. Display them together, or, with children's okay, collate them into a group book and make up a title. Place it in your library corner so children can "read" it on their own.

Remember

▪ Fours have vivid imaginations. This kind of activity will appeal to them greatly and can encourage lots of language, both oral and written. Accept whatever children say to encourage free expression.

BOOKS

| Here are books with delightful talking animal characters. | ▪ *Frog and Toad* by Arnold Lobel (Scholastic) | ▪ *Little Bear* by Else Homelund Minarik (Scholastic) | ▪ *Monty* by James Stevenson (Scholastic) |

ACTIVITY PLAN
READY-TO-USE TEACHING IDEAS FOR FOURS

abc LANGUAGE

Inspire young artists to create their own versions of a classic children's book.

LITTLE BLUE AND LITTLE YELLOW II

Aim: Children will use listening, speaking, reading, writing, and fine-motor skills and creative expression.

Group size: Four or five children.

Materials: Blue and yellow tempera paint, liquid detergent, clean plastic squeeze bottles, white drawing paper and markers; and a copy of *Little Blue and Little Yellow* by Leo Lionni (Astor).

In Advance: Fill the plastic bottles with tempera paint. Add a few drops of liquid detergent to thicken the paint, to keep it from coming out too quickly.

GETTING READY

Share with children the book *Little Blue and Little Yellow* or show the movie version of the story (distributed by Weston Woods). You can also use the following short synopsis to present the story on a flannel board. Provide time for children to share their reactions.

A blob of blue paint and a blob of yellow are friends. They hug and gradually merge into two green blobs. Together they have many adventures, but when it's time to go home, their families are upset because they don't recognize Little Blue and Little Yellow anymore. The friends cry themselves back to their original colors — and then live happily ever after.

BEGIN

Invite interested children to create their own Little Blue and Little Yellow pictures. Provide white drawing paper and the bottles of yellow and blue paint. Observe as children freely create

their pictures. Watch for places where paint may be overlapping on children's papers. Is a new color forming? Is this Little Blue and Little Yellow hugging, or just shaking hands? Be sure to let children make up their own explanations. Let each child make as many pictures as he or she wants.

Make a Class Book

When the pictures are dry, invite each child to choose one to place in a group book about Little Blue and Little Yellow. To help children imagine what might be happening to the paint characters in their pictures, you might ask, "What do you think Little Blue and Little Yellow are doing? Where might they be going? What do you think they're feeling?" Write each child's exact words on a separate sheet of paper.

Compile the pictures and dictations into a book. As you order the pages, be sure each child's words are opposite his picture, so that each child's page becomes one vignette about Little Blue and Little Yellow. Share the finished book at storytime.

Remember

▪ Don't worry if your book doesn't have a logical sequence. Pressuring children to do the book in a specific way will inhibit their creativity. Children may say what they sense you want them to say, not what's coming from their own imaginations.

▪ Use this same approach with other favorite children's stories, especially those that are illustrated in a simple style.

BOOKS

These books will inspire other great art activities.

▪ *It Looked Like Spilled Milk* by Charles Snow (Harper & Row)

▪ *Let's Make Rabbits* by Leo Lionni (Pantheon)

▪ *Splish, Splash!* by Yvonne Hooker (Grosset & Dunlap)

Here's a fun way for fours to experiment with sounds.

SHAKE A SOUND

Aim: Children will use listening, speaking, reading, and gross-motor skills in an auditory activity.

Group size: Three or four children.

Materials: Containers with lids, such as margarine tubs and coffee cans; items to make loud and soft sounds, such as gravel, plastic-foam pieces, seeds, buttons, paper clips, bells, and small balls; recordings of loud and soft music; and chart paper and markers.

GETTING READY

Ask children to listen for sounds — in the room, outside, or in their own bodies. On chart paper, list all the sounds they name. Draw a simple figure beside each word as a visual clue. Then discuss the list. Ask children to help you identify sounds that are loud and those that are soft. Spark imaginations by asking, "What do you think is the loudest sound in the world? What's the softest sound?" Encourage lots of sharing.

BEGIN

Show children the different materials you have gathered. Encourage them to predict which materials will make loud sounds and which will make soft sounds. Write their predictions on chart paper.

Now invite each child to take a container, then to choose a material to put inside it that he or she thinks will make a soft sound. Observe as fours experiment by shaking the containers. Together, check the predictions about which materials would make soft sounds. Then ask children to choose a material that they think will make a loud sound. Experiment to test their guesses.

Let children freely experiment with the materials. Observe and listen to the kinds of discoveries they report. Encourage them to try new ways of shaking their containers to see if they can vary the sounds the objects make. Invite fours to look for other objects in the room to test in their containers.

Add a Song

Play a recording of loud, fast music. Help children fill their containers with a material to make a loud, fast noise to go with the music. Then play soft, slow music. Observe and help as children choose a soft-sounding material to shake slowly to the music.

Remember

▪ Be very careful with the small items that you offer to children to

use in their shakers. Items that are smaller than a choke tube (or the size of a child's hand when made into a fist) can be dangerous if swallowed accidentally.

▪ Discriminating between sounds is an important skill that prepares children for recognizing the sounds that different letters make. Try these activities often.

BOOKS

Here are more exciting books about sounds.	▪ *A Crowd of Crows* by John Graham (Scholastic)	▪ *Plink, Plink, Plink* by Byron Baylor (Houghton Mifflin)	▪ *Too Much Noise* by Ann McGovern (Scholastic)

LANGUAGE

It's fun for fives to talk about how much they've grown!

WHEN I WAS A BABY ...

Aim: Children will use listening, speaking, reading, writing, and thinking skills as they compare their abilities now with when they were babies.

Group size: Three or four children.

Materials: Ethnically diverse baby dolls; doll furniture such as a high chair, cradle, and stroller; baby items such as a bathing basin, washcloth, diapers, bottles, spoons, unbreakable baby-food jars, and baby clothes; and chart paper and markers.

GETTING READY

Most of the baby dolls and baby items will already be in your dramatic-play area, but add any new ones you've gathered and observe the themes and activities that evolve. What actions or sounds do children associate with babies? At moments when you won't interrupt play, ask questions such as, "How do you take care of your baby?" "When will your baby be able to feed herself?" "Why is Baby crying?" As children respond, listen for comments related to a baby's abilities or needs compared with their own.

BEGIN

Gather a small group in front of two pieces of chart paper. Print "Babies can ... " on one and "I can ..." on the other. Read the first phrase aloud to children and invite them to complete the sentence. Write each child's exact response on the chart paper, then read all the responses about babies.

Read the phrase "I can ..." and invite children to take turns completing it. Write each child's exact words on the second sheet of chart paper, rereading the list when it's complete.

Compare the two charts, rereading items from the baby list as needed. Show your pride in children's increasing abilities: "Wow, look at all the things you can do now that you couldn't do when you were a baby!" Encourage fives to share other ways they know they are getting to be "big kids." Invite children to also predict what they think they'll be able to do when they are six. Write their ideas on a third sheet of chart paper you've titled "Soon I will be able to ..." Accept children's ideas, even if they are unrealistic.

Place all the charts where children can illustrate them as they wish. Display where children can "read" them on their own and share them with family members.

Invite a Baby to Visit

Extend the discussion by inviting parents with babies to visit your program. Discuss with mothers and fathers ahead of time whether they're comfortable letting fives hold and help dress, bathe, or change the babies, so you know how to encourage your children. Listen for the kinds of observations children make of baby behaviors. Ask, "Would you like to be a baby again? What do you like about being five years old?"

Remember

■ This is a great activity to do when one or more children are expecting and/or coping with new siblings at home. Remember, too, that children with new siblings may regress and act out baby-like behaviors.

BOOKS

Share these books about babies at storytime.

■ *Books Are for Eating* by Sherry Walton (E.P. Dutton)

■ *Let Me Tell You About My Baby* by Roslyn Banish (Harper & Row)

■ *When I Was a Baby* by Catherine Anholt (Little, Brown)

LANGUAGE

Create your own book based on a favorite song.

WRITE A CLASS BIG BOOK

Aim: Children will use listening, speaking, reading, and writing skills and creative expression in a cooperative activity.

Group size: Three or four children.

Materials: Chart paper and markers, large sheets of white drawing paper, crayons and markers, a stapler, construction paper, and cardboard (for cover); and a big book.

In Advance: Look for a story version of "I Know an Old Lady Who Swallowed a Fly," such as one by Rose Bonne and Abner Graboff (Scholastic).

GETTING READY

Read a story version of "I Know an Old Lady Who Swallowed a Fly" to children, and/or sing the song together. After you read, sing, and discuss the old lady's humorous predicament, invite children to change the characters to create a story of their own. Write their ideas on chart paper as they choose possible new characters and actions.

For example, children might change the old lady to a character called Poor Pig or Big Cat. Encourage them to think of new things for this character to swallow. Poor Pig might swallow only objects that start with "P," such as pizza, pears, and a piano.

Now invite children to create their own oversized book about their new character's adventures. Look through a big book you have in the room. Invite children to tell you how a big book is like a regular book and how it is different. Together, make a list of the materials children will need to make the group big book.

BEGIN

Give each child a sheet of large drawing paper to use in making one page of the book. Ask each to choose one object for the character to swallow, and to draw the character and item — or the character with the item in its stomach — on the page. Remind children to save room at the bottom of each page for some words.

Work with the children to create a rhyme to go on each page. For example: "I know a poor pig who swallowed a tie ... He said it was almost as good as a pie." When all of the children have contributed a page, decide together on a surprise ending to the book: for instance, "He's full, of course!"

Complete the book by stapling or tying all the pages together. Ask a few interested children to create a cover from the cardboard, using markers, paint, or collage materials as decoration.

Set up the group big book on an easel and enjoy it together at storytime. Then place it in your library corner so children can continue to enjoy it on their own.

Remember
- Let children create the pictures in their own ways. Unless the group has decided that the character will swallow only certain types of objects, let children be creative in choosing the objects to draw, too.

BOOKS

Here are excellent predictable books to share with fives.

- *Brown Bear, Brown Bear, What Do You See?* by Bill Martin Jr. (Henry Holt)

- *The Farmer in the Dell* by Mary Maki Rae (Scholastic)

- *"I Can't," Said the Ant* by Polly Cameron (Scholastic)

LANGUAGE

Sharpen listening skills as pairs create unusual pictures.

FOLLOW-THE-LEADER PICTURES

Aim: Children will use listening, speaking, and fine-motor skills and creative expression as they cooperate in an art activity.
Group size: Two children.
Materials: Easels and easel paper, tempera paint, and brushes.

GETTING READY

Play listening games at circle time. Start with a familiar game like Simon Says. Play it in a non-competitive way so that everyone can keep participating. Ask children to take turns being the leader, and encourage the followers to listen carefully. Or play a clapping game. As the leader claps a rhythm, the group imitates it. Vary the length and difficulty of the patterns to help children focus on listening.

BEGIN

This is a good activity to suggest when you notice that interest in easel painting is waning. It might also encourage a child who seldom paints at the easel to take a turn.

Invite two children to paint together while playing a "follow-the-leader" listening game. Demonstrate what to do by having the children take turns telling you what shapes to paint as you work at an easel. Follow their verbal directions exactly, so that children recognize that you are listening to their words and using them to create a painting.

Now have the pair each take a role — leader or follower. Ask each to stand on opposite sides of one easel (if your arrangement allows). The leader slowly paints lines and shapes on his or her paper, while giving the other child instructions to make the same lines and shapes. For example, the leader might say, "I'm painting a long blue line. Now I'm painting a big red circle." The follower listens and tries to create the same picture.

When the leader is finished, the two will naturally want to compare results. Listen as they comment on what they see. Ask, "How are your paintings the same? How are they different?" Talk about whether it's easy or hard to follow someone else's directions.

Invite the pair to switch roles and create another set of pictures. Talk about these results, too.

Remember
▪ Let the leader create whatever she wants to make. Some children will stick with lines and shapes, while others will direct the follower to "make a flower."
▪ Encourage children to try this kind of activity in other areas, too,

such as building block creations with one child as leader and one as follower, or making a snack together, with one giving the directions and one listening and cooking.

BOOKS

| Here are some special books to listen to. | ▪ *A Fly Went By* by Mike McClintock (Random House) | ▪ *The Happy Owls* by Piatti (Atheneum) | ▪ *A Kiss for Little Bear* by Else Homelund Minarik (Harper & Row) |

LANGUAGE

Fives will have many opportunities to use language skills as they create a newspaper.

THE KINDERGARTEN TIMES

Aim: Children will use listening, speaking, reading, and writing skills in a cooperative activity.

Group size: Small or large groups.

Materials: A newspaper (*USA Today* is a good choice because it has so many pictures), chart paper, white paper, crayons and markers, and empty paper-towel rolls.

GETTING READY

Show a real newspaper to children. Ask, "What is in a newspaper? Why do people read a newspaper?" Listen to children's ideas and experiences with family members reading the newspaper. Explain that newspapers are used to tell people about events that are happening where they live and in faraway places, too.

Go through the paper and identify parts children can relate to, such as photographs that help tell stories, comics, sports, puzzles, advertisements, and weather forecasts. Choose an article that children will find interesting and share a summarized version with them.

BEGIN

Invite children to create a newspaper. Put up a blank sheet of chart paper and explain that you'll use one sheet for each "section" of the newspaper. You might start with a page titled "Weather." Invite children to share "reports" of what the weather is like today. Write their words as they dictate them. For example: "Weatherperson Jack says it is cold out today." "Weatherperson Abby says there is snow on the ground." Invite children to predict what the weather will be like tomorrow. "Weatherperson Matt says it will snow 100 inches tomorrow!" Later, invite children to illustrate the page.

Do an "interview" for the paper by inviting a familiar person, such as the cook or bus driver, to speak to the group. Before your guest arrives, ask children to suggest questions they'd like to ask about the person's job, family, or favorite activities, such as, "What do you like to cook best?" "Did you go to preschool?" Write the questions on chart paper. As children ask these questions of the visitor, summarize the response below each question. Children might also fashion "microphones" from empty paper-towel rolls to interview the guest like TV reporters.

Put Your Book Together

Continue this activity over several days, as long as children's interest holds. You might create pages on projects, children's news from home, comics, etc. Provide paper, crayons, and markers so children can illustrate the pages. When the newspaper is complete, decide together on a name for it to add to the top of the first page. Staple the pages together, share this first edition as a group, and then add it to the library corner.

Remember

▪ Fives enjoy long-term projects. Some children may want to set up a "newspaper office" in your theme center. Stock it with paper, markers, a typewriter, stamps and stamp pads, and a telephone.

▪ Plan a field trip to a real newspaper office before or after you create your class newspaper.

BOOKS

Try these books for information about reporting the news.

▪ *Little Store on the Corner* by Alice P. Miller (Scholastic)

▪ *Too Hot in Potzburg* by Seymour Fleishman (Albert Whitman)

▪ *What Can She Be? A Newscaster* by Gloria Goldreic (Lothrop, Lee & Shepard)

LANGUAGE

Turn a neighborhood walk into an alphabet scavenger hunt!

LET'S TAKE A LETTER WALK

Aim: Children will use listening, speaking, reading, writing, observing, matching, and motor skills as they hunt for letters and numbers in everyday places.

Group size: Whole class or small groups.

Materials: Letter and numeral cards (see below), thin newsprint paper, and old crayons.

In Advance: Print the letters of the alphabet on individual file cards, one letter per card, as well as numerals from one to 10 on separate cards. Choose letters that children are familiar with and which can be found on many signs in your area.

GETTING READY

Show children the letter and numeral cards and talk about letter and number names. Start with a letter hunt inside. Ask children to look around the room and point out the letters and numbers they see.

If children enjoy this activity, invite them to widen their search by taking a walk outdoors to look for letters and numerals in signs, on buildings, etc. You might give each child one or two cards to make his or her special letters or numerals to look for on the walk. (Be sure everyone knows they can look for all letters and numerals, not just the ones on their cards.)

BEGIN

Follow a route that offers many signs, buildings, or vehicles with letters and numerals on them. Occasionally stop and try to figure out the meaning of familiar signs together. Talk about which letters children seem to see most often.

Make Letter Rubbings

Take along thin newsprint paper and unwrapped crayons on your walk. Look for signs that have raised letters and show children how to place the paper over the letters and gently rub the side of the crayon on the paper so the letters or numerals appear.

Remember

▪ Some children will be able to match the letters on cards to the letters on signs, but won't know the names of the letters. That connection will come with concrete experiences like this one, especially if children don't feel rushed.

▪ Knowing the order of the letters of the alphabet isn't a concrete learning experience for children this age. It is more age-appropriate for children to begin to recognize signs, words, and letters that are closest to them, such as a STOP sign or letters in their name.

▪ Safety is important on a high-activity walk like this one. Be sure you have enough adults so that someone is watching every child.

BOOKS

Enjoy these interesting alphabet books before and after your walk.

▪ *A, B, See!* by Tana Hoban (Greenwillow Books)

▪ *Alfred's Alphabet Walk* by Victoria Chess (Greenwillow Books)

▪ *Alphabet World* by Barry Miller (Macmillan)

a b c	LANGUAGE

Help fives understand the passage of time.

"MY DAY" BOOKS

Aim: Children will use listening, speaking, reading, writing, fine-motor, and sequencing skills as they describe and order events in their day.

Group size: Four or five children.

Materials: Toy clock, white drawing paper, construction paper, crayons, markers, stapler, glue, magazine pictures, and scissors.

In Advance: Invite a few children to help you prepare blank books. Use construction paper for covers and fill each book with four blank pages.

GETTING READY

Show children a toy clock. Let them handle it and point the hands to different hours. Talk about how a clock helps people know what time of day it is. Ask, "What tells you that a new day is starting? What do you see or do that tells you that a day is over?" Listen to children's comments and ideas. Point out that most people do certain activities at particular times of the day, like eating breakfast in the morning.

Invite children to brainstorm a list of all the things they do in the morning. Record these on a chart marked with a rising sun. Next, have children suggest things they do and see in the afternoon, and create a full sun on this page. Finally, ask children to name things they do and see at night. Mark this chart with a crescent moon. Review the lists together.

BEGIN

Give children the blank "My Day" books. Invite them to fill the pages with activities they do each day. Post the charts to help with ideas and with writing words. To reinforce sequencing skills, ask children to follow a special order: The first page is for things they do before they come to your setting. The second is for activities during your program. The third is for what they do after they go home. The fourth page is for nighttime activities.

Provide art materials and magazine pictures for children to use to picture and describe the events. Encourage them to "write" and draw their thoughts on each page. Some children may prefer to dictate words for you to write on the pages. Finish by helping each child write a title on the book cover. Then invite children to share their books with others.

Make a Time-Sequence Card Game

Ask children to look through magazines for pictures of events that happen throughout a day. Have them cut or tear out pictures, then glue them onto large index cards (five inches by seven inches). Shuffle the cards and invite children to sequence them from morning (left) to night (right).

Remember

▪ Work shifts and other factors may mean some families will have non-traditional routines. Breakfast foods may be served as evening meals in some homes. Be accepting of the events which children choose to represent each time of day.

▪ Time is still an abstract concept for children this age. Concrete activities like this one can help to further their understanding.

BOOKS

Take time to share these books with children.	▪ *The King's Tea* by Trinka Hakes Noble (Dial Books)	▪ *The Man Who Tried to Save Time* by Phyllis Krasilovsky (Doubleday)	▪ *On Sunday the Wind Came* by Alan C. Elliot (William Morrow & Co.)

a b c LANGUAGE

As popcorn bursts, so will language!

POPCORN PREDICTIONS

Aim: Children will use listening, speaking, observation, prediction, and comparison skills while preparing a popcorn snack.
Group size: Four or five children.
Materials: Kernels of corn to pop, bowl of popped corn, chart paper and marker, popcorn popper (oil or hot air), clean mural paper, crayons, small bowls, and napkins.

GETTING READY

Pass around bowls of popped and unpopped corn for children to look at, feel, and smell. Let children snack on the popped corn as they brainstorm a list of everything they know about it. Record their comments on chart paper. Encourage them to share descriptive words like *white*, *soft*, *buttery*, and *crunchy*.

BEGIN

Talk about what a prediction is, giving children time to share their ideas. Help them understand that a prediction is like a guess. Then invite children to make predictions about popcorn.

Place a large sheet of clean mural paper on the floor. Put the popcorn popper in the center of the paper. As a safety precaution, leave about four to five feet of exposed paper on all sides of the popper.

Gather children in a circle around the outside of the paper. Explain that today they are going to pop the popcorn without a lid on the popper. Ask children to guess what they think will happen when the lid is kept off. Ask, "How far do you think the popcorn will jump out of the popper?" Invite each child to draw a small circle to represent his or her prediction. Help children write their names or initials by their circles.

Time to start popping! For safety, fill the popper with half the amount of kernels normally called for. Half will still be fun and you won't have to wait as long to insure all kernels have popped. Watch children carefully to be sure they stand back from the popper. Remind them that the kernels are very hot.

When the popcorn stops popping, take a few minutes to check your predictions. Ask, "Do you think your predictions would be closer if we tried this activity again?" Give children time to share their ideas. Talk about how predictions get better when you have some information to base them on. Repeat the prediction activity another day. Or make another batch with the lid on to enjoy as a snack while sharing a book about popcorn.

Remember

▪ Do try this activity several times with fives to help them see how their ability to make predictions improves with practice.
▪ As a creative extension, invite small groups to make up a story about what would happen if your popper would not stop popping popcorn. Record the story on chart paper, and let children illustrate it with crayons or markers. Share it with the whole group, and display it where children can "read" it on their own.

BOOKS

We predict children will love these books about popcorn!	▪ *Mr. Picklepaw's Popcorn* by Ruth Adams (Lothrop, Lee & Shepard)	▪ *Popcorn* by Milicent Selsam (William Morrow & Co.)	▪ *The Popcorn Book* by Tomie dePaola (Holiday House)

a b c LANGUAGE

A classic children's story can lead to wonderful flights of fancy!

A TRIP TO MONSTER MOUNTAIN

Aim: Children will use listening, speaking, and gross-motor skills and creative expression.

Group size: Whole group.

Materials: Carpet squares (for "magic carpets"), a recording of "flying" music (such as from "Peter Pan"), a box or a large hollow or foam block; and *Where the Wild Things Are* by Maurice Sendak (Harper & Row).

GETTING READY

Gather children to read aloud *Where the Wild Things Are*, sharing the illustrations. After you read, talk about monsters. Listen to children's comments, and reassure wary fives that there are no such things as the monsters in this book.

Invite children to take an imaginary trip to Monster Mountain, a place where friendly monsters live. Ask, "What do you think Monster Mountain looks like? What do the monsters who live there like to do?" Provide plenty of time for everyone to share ideas.

BEGIN

Give a carpet square to each child, then ask how the group might use these squares to get to Monster Mountain. Some children may introduce the idea of "flying carpets," but let them use the carpets in whatever imaginative ways they devise.

Ask children to find a space on the floor for their carpets. Suggest a chant to start the carpets: "Hands in the air and hands on your nose. Touch the carpet and off it goes! VROOM! WHOOSH!" Invite children to make their own sound effects, too.

Now play the music and ask children to move like they are flying to Monster Mountain. Talk about what they see along the way and how it feels to fly. When the music stops, guide everyone to a safe landing.

Sing a Monster-Mountain Song

Place a box or block in the center of the group. Tell children that they're at the bottom of Monster Mountain and they have to climb it to visit the friendly monsters. Sing this song to the tune of "The Bear Went Over the Mountain":

> **The Monster Went Over the Mountain**
> *The monster went over the mountain*
> *The monster went over the mountain*
> *The monster went over the mountain*
> *To see what he (she) could see.*

Encourage children to describe what they see on Monster Mountain. When interest starts to wane, repeat the chant to fly your carpets home.

Remember

▪ You can take another flight to Monster Mountain outdoors. The jungle gym or slide can be the mountain that everyone climbs.

▪ Provide puppet-making materials to extend this activity. Interested children can use old, clean socks and material scraps to create friendly monsters for dramatizing the Sendak story or one of their own.

BOOKS

| Rest from your adventure with another monster book. | ▪ *Boris and the Monsters* by Elaine Willoughby (Houghton Mifflin) | ▪ *Harry and the Terrible Whatzit* by Dick Gackenbach (Houghton Mifflin) | ▪ *How Do You Hide a Monster?* by Virgina Kahl (Scholastic) |

LANGUAGE Introduce personal poetry with a familiar nursery rhyme!

CREATE A NURSERY RHYME

Aim: Children will use listening, speaking, reading, and writing skills in a creative activity.

Group size: Three or four children.

Materials: Chart paper, markers and crayons, a few seashells and small bells, and metal ring binders.

In Advance: Copy the nursery rhyme "Mary, Mary," below, onto chart paper. Print clearly and leave space between the lines. Invite a few interested children to draw pictures on the chart to go with the words.

> *Mary, Mary, quite contrary,*
> *How does your garden grow?*
> *With silver bells and cockle shells,*
> *And pretty maids all in a row.*

GETTING READY

Show children the chart and say the rhyme together several times. Talk about the words in the rhyme. Ask, "What are silver bells and cockle shells?" Pass around some seashells and silver bells for children to hold and describe. Have they ever seen anyone growing bells or shells in a garden? Talk about where children have seen bells and shells before. What funny things would children grow in a garden of their own? Give the group plenty of time to share their ideas.

BEGIN

Invite children to use their ideas in new versions of this nursery rhyme that feature their own names. For example, instead of "Mary, Mary, quite contrary," substitute, "Jesse, Jesse, Jesse Smith." After "How does your garden grow?" ask the child to choose the items he or she would like to grow in a garden. Enlist others in the group to help if a child is struggling to find a word that rhymes with *grow*. Then share the new poem together aloud:

> *Jesse, Jesse, Jesse Smith*
> *How does your garden grow?*
> *With shiny trucks and tiny cars*
> *Riding all in a row!*

Write each child's rhyme on chart paper, and let him decorate the page.

Make a Big Book

Collect the finished rhymes and put them together in a group book. Laminate the pages for durability, then secure with metal ring binders. (Children will be turning the pages frequently, so it's best to be prepared for all this loving use.) By reading the poems over and over, you'll help children quickly memorize each other's poems, and they'll learn their peers' first and last names, too!

Remember

■ Don't insist that children substitute phrases that rhyme. Most will want to because they like the sound of the rhyming words. But accept whatever words children give you.

■ Repeat this activity with other favorite nursery rhymes. Create a whole library of personalized poems!

BOOKS

Here are good collections of nursery rhymes.

■ *The Arbuthnot Anthology of Children's Literature* by Zena Sutherland (Scott, Foresman & Co.)

■ *The Faber Book of Nursery Verse* by Barbara Iveson (Faber and Faber)

■ *A Treasure of Mother Goose* by Hilda Offen (Simon & Schuster)

a b c	LANGUAGE	**Here's a delightful way to combine music and language.**

ORCHESTRATE A FAVORITE STORY

Aim: Children will use listening, speaking, music, motor, and creative-thinking skills as they "play along" with a familiar story.
Group size: Whole group or small groups.
Materials: Rhythm instruments such as triangles, tambourines, bells, and wooden sticks; chart paper and markers; and a popular repetitive story, such as one listed below, that features several characters.

GETTING READY

Read or tell the story you've chosen to children. Discuss the different characters and what they do. Note the specific traits of the characters: big or small, young or old, good or bad. Record the character names and their traits on chart paper.

Introduce the collection of rhythm instruments. Give children time to play with them and to listen to the different sounds they make.

BEGIN

Now invite children to help you retell the story using the rhythm instruments. Name one character in the story and review the character's traits from your chart. Then ask children to decide on a rhythm instrument with a sound that fits that character. For example, in *The Three Billy Goats Gruff*, the biggest goat might be represented by a drum and the smallest by a bell. Draw a simple outline of the instrument chosen for each character next to the character's name on the chart. Let children each choose a character to "play" on a rhythm instrument.

If there are more children than characters, invite other children to make sound effects to go with the story. For example, a child with wooden blocks could make the sound of the goats clomping over the bridge.

Seat children with similar instruments together. Explain that you will read the story again. Each time a child hears his character's name, he makes a quick sound with his instrument. Remind children to listen very carefully so they know when to play.

Now retell the story, pausing as you name characters or actions that children have been assigned. Repeat the activity if children's interest is high, inviting them to trade instruments and characters.

Orchestrate a Song

This same procedure can be used with a repetitive song, too. Try an old favorite like "The Wheels on the Bus" or "Old MacDonald." Help children choose instruments to represent objects, animals, or people. As children sing, have them play their instrument when they hear their cue words.

Remember

■ Emphasize the fun of this activity over perfect orchestration of words and instruments. It's a great listening exercise, but children will miss much of the enjoyment if they're worried about making mistakes.
■ Place the rhythm instruments where small groups of children can dramatize the same story (or another) themselves or with puppets, and include the instruments as part of the dramatization.

BOOKS

| Try orchestrating these versions of old favorites. | ■ *The House That Jack Built* by Paul Galdone (McGraw-Hill) | ■ *Stone Soup* by Marcia Brown (Scholastic) | ■ *The Three Billy Goats Gruff* by Peter Christian Asbjorsen (Harcourt Brace Jovanovich) |

ACTIVITY PLAN INDEX:
TWOS AND THREES

DEVELOPMENTAL AREAS AND SKILLS ENHANCED	LANGUAGE SKILLS					OTHER AREAS						
	LISTENING	SPEAKING	READING	WRITING	CREATIVE EXPRESSION	DRAMATIC PLAY	SCIENCE/MATH CONCEPTS	PROBLEM-SOLVING SKILLS	COOPERATING/ SHARING	EXPRESSING EMOTIONS	FINE-MOTOR SKILLS	GROSS-MOTOR SKILLS
2'S ACTIVITY PLANS												
TAKING CARE OF ME PAGE 38	■	■		■		■		■		■	■	
LET'S GO FOR A RIDE! PAGE 39	■	■				■		■		■	■	
HAVING FUN WITH LANGUAGE PAGE 40	■	■									■	
FINGER PUPPETS AND FINGERPLAYS PAGE 41	■	■			■					■	■	
WHAT'S OUTSIDE OUR WINDOW? PAGE 42	■	■	■	■			■			■		
WHO IS THIS? PAGE 43	■	■	■	■						■		
MAKING APPLESAUCE PAGE 44	■	■	■				■		■		■	
EXPERIENCING COLOR PAGE 45	■	■	■		■		■	■		■	■	
EXPLORING THE DARK! PAGE 46	■	■	■				■	■		■	■	
LISTEN TO THE BIRDS PAGE 47	■	■	■	■			■			■		
3'S ACTIVITY PLANS												
TALKING ON THE TELEPHONE PAGE 48	■	■	■	■		■			■	■	■	
FOLLOW THE "TEXTURE ROAD" PAGE 49	■	■			■		■		■	■	■	
LET'S PLAY CIRCLE GAMES! PAGE 50	■	■								■		
ANIMAL RHYMES PAGE 51	■	■			■		■	■		■	■	
TAKE A LISTENING WALK PAGE 52	■	■			■		■	■		■		
TALKING "TINY" TALK PAGE 53	■	■	■	■	■		■			■		
THE GO-TOGETHER GAME PAGE 54	■	■					■	■	■			
ALL MY FRIENDS AND FAMILY PAGE 55	■	■		■						■	■	
WHAT'S THAT SOUND? PAGE 56	■	■						■	■		■	
MUSHING, GUSHING, AND TALKING PAGE 57												

ACTIVITY PLAN INDEX:
FOURS AND FIVES

DEVELOPMENTAL AREAS AND SKILLS ENHANCED	LANGUAGE SKILLS					OTHER AREAS						
	Listening	Speaking	Reading	Writing	Creative Expression	Dramatic Play	Science/Math Concepts	Problem-Solving Skills	Cooperating/Sharing	Expressing Emotions	Fine-Motor Skills	Gross-Motor Skills
4'S ACTIVITY PLANS												
"IN THE DARK, DARK ..." PAGE 58	■	■	■	■	■	■			■	■	■	
RHYME AND RHYTHM PAGE 59	■	■	■	■	■					■		■
LOTS AND LOTS OF SHOES PAGE 60	■	■	■	■	■	■	■	■	■			■
SOCK IT TO ME! PAGE 61	■	■	■	■	■					■	■	
HOLA MEANS *HELLO* PAGE 62	■	■	■	■	■				■	■	■	■
OUR DAY AT SCHOOL PAGE 63	■	■	■	■	■		■		■	■		
TURN CARDS INTO BOOKS PAGE 64	■	■	■	■	■					■	■	
WHAT IF ANIMALS COULD TALK? PAGE 65	■	■	■	■	■		■	■		■	■	
LITTLE BLUE AND LITTLE YELLOW II PAGE 66	■	■	■	■	■		■		■	■	■	
SHAKE A SOUND PAGE 67	■	■	■	■	■		■		■	■	■	■
5'S ACTIVITY PLANS												
WHEN I WAS A BABY ... PAGE 68	■	■	■	■	■	■			■	■	■	
WRITE A CLASS BIG BOOK PAGE 69	■	■	■	■	■				■		■	
FOLLOW-THE-LEADER PICTURES PAGE 70	■	■			■			■	■	■	■	■
THE KINDERGARTEN TIMES PAGE 71	■	■	■	■	■	■		■	■	■	■	
LET'S TAKE A LETTER WALK PAGE 72	■		■				■		■	■	■	■
"MY DAY" BOOKS PAGE 73	■	■	■	■	■		■		■	■	■	
POPCORN PREDICTIONS PAGE 74	■	■	■	■	■		■	■	■		■	
A TRIP TO MONSTER MOUNTAIN PAGE 75	■	■			■			■	■	■	■	■
CREATE A NURSERY RHYME PAGE 76	■	■	■	■	■			■	■		■	
ORCHESTRATE A FAVORITE STORY PAGE 77												

RESOURCES

These helpful resources can offer more information and guidance on developing your children's language skills. Look for them at libraries and bookstores, or contact publishers directly for ordering information.

ARTICLES

▼ *"Books Are Just a Beginning"* by MaryJane Margini Rossi, *Pre-K Today*, January 1990

▼ *"Language Develops as Children Play"* by Sandra Waite-Stupiansky, Ph.D., *Pre-K Today*, January 1989

▼ *"Making Language Discoveries"* by Judith A. Schickedanz, *Pre-K Today*, January 1990

▼ *"Once Upon a Time ... The Art of Story Telling"* by Ellen Booth Church, *Pre-K Today*, January 1990

▼ *"Puppet Play Explores Feelings and Emotions"* by Elyse Jacobs, *Pre-K Today*, January 1989

▼ *"Reading Aloud to Children"* by Ellen Booth Church, *Pre-K Today*, January 1991

▼ *"Share a Story With Me,"* Infant/Toddler Special Feature, *Pre-K Today*, January 1990

▼ *"Storytime Is More Than Reading Books"* by Bev Bos, *Pre-K Today*, January 1989

▼ *"Whole Language: It's an Experience!"* by Susan Miller, Ed.D., *Pre-K Today*, January 1991

PROFESSIONAL BOOKS

▼ *Early Childhood Experiences in Language Arts* by Jeanne M. Manchado (Delmar Press)

▼ *Emerging Literacy: Young Children Learn to Read and Write* by Dorothy S. Strickland and Lesley Mandel Morrow (National Association for the Education of Young Children)

▼ *MORE Story Stretchers: More Activities to Expand Children's Favorite Books* by Shirley C. Raines and Robert J. Canady (Gryphon House)

▼ *Story Stretchers: Activities to Expand Children's Favorite Books* by Shirley C. Raines and Robert J. Canady (Gryphon House)

▼ *The Whole Language Catalog* by Kenneth S. Goodman, Lois Bridges Bird, and Yetta M. Goodman (American School Publishers)

▼ *The Whole Language Kindergarten* by Shirley C. Raines and Robert J. Canady (Teachers College Press)

▼ *Writing With Reason: The Emergence of Authorship in Young Children* by Nigel Hall (Heinemann Educational Books, Inc.)

FILMS AND VIDEO

▼ *Floor Time: Tuning In To Each Child,* a teacher-training program based on the work of Stanley Greenspan, M.D., for guiding children's emotional development (Scholastic Professional Development Video)

▼ *Supporting Communication Among Preschoolers,* a seven-part film series (High/Scope Press)